Shakespeare
and the Spectacles
of Strangeness

Medieval and Renaissance Literary Studies

Shakespeare and the Spectacles of Strangeness

The Tempest *and the Transformation of Renaissance Theatrical Forms*

John G. Demaray

DUQUESNE UNIVERSITY PRESS
Pittsburgh, Pennsylvania

Library of Congress Cataloging in Publication Data

Demaray, John G.
Shakespeare and the spectacles of strangeness: The tempest and the transformation of Renaissance theatrical forms / John G. Demaray.
p. cm. — (Medieval and Renaissance literary studies)
Includes index.
ISBN 0-8207-0284-6 (alk. paper)
1. Shakespeare, William, 1564-1616. Tempest. 2. Shakespeare, William, 1564-1616—Stage history—To 1625. 3. Shakespeare, William, 1564-1616—Stage history—England. 4. Great Britain—Court and courtiers—History—17th century. 5. Theater—England—History—17th century. 6. Spectacular, The, in literature. 7. Masques—History and criticism. 8. Magic in literature. 9. Literary form. I. Title. II. Series.
PR2833.D46 1997
822.3'3—dc21 97-33771
CIP

For Hannah

her Ma.[tie] (best knowing, that a principall part of life in these *Spectacles* lay in they[r] variety) had commaunded mee to think on some *Daunce*, or shew that might praecede hers, and haue the place of a foyle . . . I . . . therefore, now, deuis'd that twelue Women, in the habite of *Haggs*, or Witches . . . should fill that part; . . . not as a *Masque*, but a spectacle of strangenesse, producing multiplicity of Gesture, and not vnaptly sorting w[t]h the current, and whole fall of the Deuise.

Ben Jonson, Preface to the
Masque of Queenes (1609)

I' the name of something holy, Sir, why stand you
in this strange stare?

Gonzalo, addressing Alonso
who gazes at a visionary
spectacle

These are not naturall euents, they strengthen
From strange, to stranger

Alonso, viewing "dead"
seamen who suddenly
enter

All torment, trouble, wonder, and amazement
Inhabits heere. some heauenly power guide vs

Gonzalo, on the experience of
the magical island

Contents

Illustrations

Page

Preface

Shakespeare's *The Tempest* is a unique drama charged with the wonder of magic and rich in the evocation of the strange. The play's unusual characters, enchanted island setting, and mysterious action turning on magical spells leave a deep impression on the imagination, and yet the nature of this late, possibly last, play and its underlying symbolism have proved elusive for generations of critics. Commentators over the years have disagreed about its literary and theatrical antecedents; about its form, symbolism and genre; and about the manner of its early staging.

The design, staging allusions, and symbolism of *The Tempest* are here freshly reconsidered in the light of the drama's historical and theatrical *milieu*. This study maintains that in composing *The Tempest* Shakespeare was not primarily reverting to the "academic" dramatic structures, themes and character-types of his early career, but was forging a new kind of experimental drama from altering theatrical traditions. This type of drama encompassed the masquing Spectacle Triumph, in both its old and new forms, and emphasized reformist open symbolism rather than the classical iconography of Ben Jonson. *The Tempest* draws upon the European and English spectacle, pastoral, romance and dramatic traditions while at the same time pointing the way to the stylized heroic dramas of the Restoration with their exotic themes and staged scenic illusions. Thus

Shakespeare's play reflects Renaissance literary and theatrical forms in transition.

This study advances an innovative discussion of genre and structure. It pays close attention to matters of printing and textual scholarship. It challenges conventional critical perspectives on *The Tempest* by emphasizing the importance of the drama's documented ceremonial court performances before King James I. It calls attention to the relevance to Shakespeare's last plays of the neglected French *balet de cour* and the related continental spectacle tradition. On the basis of an examination of Revels Office Rolls in the British Public Records Office and primary documents in continental libraries, the study discusses in original ways the stage fabric and the conventions of court presentations influencing Shakespeare's theatrical references, and it provides revealing new accounts of the imaginative significance of the remarkable stage illusions designed by Inigo Jones in the early 1600s. It analyzes as well the rich symbolism of neglected reformist theatrical writers influencing Shakespeare, such as Samuel Daniel and Thomas Campion.

This study was in part stimulated by what seemed to me loose comparisons of Shakespeare's *The Tempest* and a variety of early academic plays, pastoral dramas and masques including John Milton's *A Mask presented at Ludlow Castle*, popularly known as *Comus*. These comparisons lacked an adequate awareness of shifting structural patterns and merging genres. The sheer volume of Shakespeare criticism has, of course, yielded plentiful insights into ideological themes, character types, political references, and pastoral motifs in these "transitional" works. Yet I find much recent criticism characterized by a lack of concern about, or an attempted deconstructive dismissal of, what seem to me interrelated patterns of form in *The Tempest* and other works; by a tendency to treat the play noncontextually, seizing upon a character or several passages as a vehicle for presenting theoretical views; and by a preference for citing and addressing commentators of just one's own theoretical or critical persuasion. Much contemporary commentary or "discourse" on *The Tempest* has a fragmented quality about it that this present study seeks to overcome.

This reading, while concentrating on court theatrical influences on Shakespeare's play, is indebted to strands of relevant commentary in different disciplines and critical theory. Instead of bypassing conflicting views, it seeks in both text and notes to acknowledge and to position itself within significant cross currents of historicist, new historicist, modernist and recent textual scholarship. The study accordingly attempts to dissociate, identify, and then gain full perspective on the theatrical structures and generic natures of *The Tempest*—with original interpretations of the play's design and genre introduced—so that passages can be read contextually even as external historical and textual influences and supposed subtexts are explored.

This book rests upon close reviews of First Folio printings of the *The Tempest* and of printings of dramas, masques, *balets de cour*, spectacle productions and stage documents at the British Records Office, the Cambridge University Library and British Libraries, the Bibliothèque Nationale, the Henry E. Huntington Library and the New York Public Library. It is supported by onsite investigations of the English and European locations of early productions. And it is indebted to past studies of Renaissance theatrical documents at the Cini Foundation, Venice, and Italian libraries as recorded in *Milton and the Masque Tradition* and *Milton's Theatrical Epic: The Invention and Design of Paradise Lost.*

Grateful acknowledgment is made to the National Endowment for the Humanities for a fellowship in 1994–95 to Cambridge University for the study of medieval and Early Modern travel, pilgrimage, historical, and theatrical texts—part of a work in progress on Renaissance historiography—of a kind underlying allusions in Shakespeare's plays. I am indebted also to Rutgers University for a leave arrangement during this period together with a subsequent Rutgers Research Council award in support of the present work. Thanks are due the New York Public Library for access to a rich research collection and use of the Frederic Lewis Allen

Room. Appreciated too is assistance from individual staff members of the British Library, British Public Records Office, Cambridge University Library, Globe Theatre Education Center, Bibliothèque Nationale, and, in particular, the Henry E. Huntington Library.

Scolar Press has kindly granted permission to publish a revised and enlarged version of "All . . . trouble, wonder, and 'amazement': Shakespeare's *The Tempest* and the New Courtly Hieroglyphics," appearing in *Shakespeare's Universe, Renaissance Ideas and Conventions: Essays in honour of W. B. Elton* (1996), pp. 135–43.

My warm gratitude for advice and academic assistance is extended to John M. Steadman, Cyndia Clegg, Elizabeth Truax, William B. Elton, Stanley Stewart and James Riddell. For suggestions and generous research help in England, I am especially indebted to David Cheshire of the British Theatre Trust, Jane Cunningham of the Courtauld Art Institute, British drama editor John Cavanagh, and International Shakespeare Globe Center representative Patrick Spottiswoode. Frederick Lewis Allen Room associates Elizabeth Hawes, David Lowe, Gloria Deak and Lawrence Lader are thanked for their encouragement and good counsel, as is my university associate Marian Da Vinci-Nichols. In this interdisciplinary study, I am obligated as well to the accomplished stage illusionists of the London Magic Circle and the California Magic Castle for historical perspectives and practical insights on problems in operating the levitation and other stage machines once used in English court spectacles. My thanks for very helpful academic criticism and support are here expressed to Albert C. Labriola; and for excellent editorial work, to Susan Wadsworth-Booth and Mary P. Groeninger. Any inadequacies in the completed study are entirely those of the author. As always, I once again owe my deepest obligations for constant encouragement, scholarly aid, and perceptive criticism to Hannah Disinger Demaray.

Introduction

In the well-known dedicatory verse "To the memory of my beloued, The Avthor, Mr. William Shakespeare," Ben Jonson, introducing the 1623 Folio of Shakespeare's plays, paid tribute to Shakespeare using a curious and generally neglected metaphor. Jonson, in praising the playwright and the British theatre, presents Shakespeare as a participant in a Triumph, a theatrical form characterized by the surprise entry and revelatory unmasking of disguised aristocrats.

> *Triumph my* Britaine, *thou hast one to showe,*
> *To whom all scenes of* Europe homage owe[1]

As the leading author of English court masques in the early 1600s, Jonson would have known that Shakespeare himself presented such Triumphs in masque-like sequences in his plays. Now Jonson imaginatively transforms Shakespeare into the main performer in just such an unmasking.

But first, Jonson proclaims the playwright unequaled among even the most notable English poets and dramatists; and in extraordinary and famed homage to Shakespeare and his work, Jonson, a classicist, declares that proper "honor" can be bestowed only by calling "To life againe" the greatest authors of antiquity and history:

> . . . *thund'ring* Aeschilus
> Euripides, *and* Sophocles *to us,*
> Paccuulius, Accius, *him of* Cordoua *dead*

Then a personified Britain presents the featured playwright-performer before an imagined stage spectacle showing "*all Scenes of* Europe." Coming directly forward in the fashion of a main masquer making an entry, Shakespeare is at once recognized as an exalted master of theatrical arts who charms and warms his audiences; for the playwright appears like one of the traditional masquing figures, the gods of music or dance, who were regularly seen on the court stage directing ordered groups of singers and dancers.

> *And all the* Muses *still were in their prime,*
> *when like* Apollo *he came forth to warme*
> *Our eares, or like a* Mercury *to charme!*

Shakespeare also assumes a theatrical-literary role similar to that of court masque and costume designer Inigo Jones. Shakespeare, Jonson writes, is the designer of the linguistic costumes worn by Nature, another traditional masque figure who by convention donned and doffed iconographic colored robes on stage to signify the changing of the seasons.

> *Nature her selfe was proud of his designes*
> *And ioy'd to weare the dressing of his lines!*
> *which were so richly spun, and wouen so fit,*
> *As, since, she will vouchsafe no other Wit*

But unlike the evanescent triumphs in main masques nostalgically described by Jonson in notes to *Hymenaei* (1606), the revelation of William Shakespeare will not be comparable to the paper-and-canvas fabric of a staged theatrical vision, one momentarily shown and then forever gone. The revelation will be enduring. "*He was not of an age,*" Jonson writes in the next line, "*but for all time!*"

Jonson's unusual tribute to Shakespeare clearly arises from the specific theatrical milieu of the early 1600s. The figure Britain had appeared as a character in Anthony Mundy's *The Triumphs of a Re-United Britain*, a London pageant presented on 29 October 1605 "to solemmize" Sir Leonard Holliday's "entrance as Lorde Mayor of the Citty."[2] In the 1620s and 1630s the term Triumph—one usually applied to entries and unmaskings—was being used by Jonson and others in the titles of masques that celebrated a personified, victorious Britain; namely, Jonson's *Neptune's Triumph* for the returne of Albion (1624); Aurelian Townshend's *Albion's Triumph* (1632), and William Davenant's *Britannia Triumphans* (1638). In 1613 during the year when *The Tempest* was staged at court, the figure Europe played a role in Thomas Campion's *Somerset's Masque* appearing "in the habit of an Empresse, with an Emperiall Crowne on her head."[3]

In Jonson's couplet, victorious Britain, presenting the featured figure Shakespeare, has by implication transcended the tragic, for masques celebrated the victory of princes rather than their fall. But most importantly, Jonson's metaphor provides an authoritative clue to a central, defining, but still neglected feature of Shakespeare's festive drama. The metaphor of Triumph appears in the Folio of 1623 only four pages—that is, two leaf pages—before the play with which it can be most closely associated: *The Tempest*, a drama in which Shakespeare presents his most innovative theatrical adaptations of masque and Triumph conventions. Although probably written last by Shakespeare, *The Tempest* was nevertheless placed first in the collection. And the printed text of the play, divided into five acts containing a total of nine scenes, shows evidence of having been set out with considerably greater care than many of the early comedies and middle-period tragedies.

Problems in interpreting *The Tempest* arise in part from problems in assessing its elusive genre, its basic theatrical structures, its mode of initial stage presentation, and the performance site or sites for which it was probably intended.

These issues remain very much open for analysis; critical assumptions on these and related matters have been shaped for too long by a massive body of editions and published works that stress assumed but undocumented early productions of the drama indoors at the Blackfriars playhouse and outdoors at the Globe. These works give only minimal attention to the quite different production of the drama before the king at Whitehall.

The present study takes another path. So strong is the presumption that *The Tempest* was written for presentation with some traps and wires at Blackfriars or perhaps at the Globe, a presumption discussed at some length in chapter 3, that a further examination of alternative or complementary views is very much needed. Ben Jonson's unusual metaphor extolling Shakespeare in a masque-like Triumph should thus serve as a reminder of basic facts concerning the site of the earliest productions of the play.

The first documented performance of *The Tempest* took place in the presence of King James at court, almost certainly in the Masquing House, on the evening of 1 November 1611 just after All Hallows Eve when demonic spirits were believed to roam the earth. On "Hollomas nyght," the *Revels Account* for 1611 reads, "Was presented at Whitehall before the Kinges Maiestie a play called The Tempest."[4] At this same period in October 1611, an Audit Office Account notes a payment "To James Maxwell gentleman usher . . . for making ready . . . the Banqueting House there at Whitehall three several tymes for playes";[5] and it was in late October and early November that the King's Men, the company that included Shakespeare, presented just three plays at court: *The Winter's Tale, The Tempest,* and a third drama with a title that went unlisted.

The second and the only other documented performance of the play in Shakespeare's lifetime was again before King James at Whitehall in 1613 in celebration of the marriage of the King's daughter, Princess Elizabeth, to Frederick Elector of Palatine, a Protestant prince noted for his occultist views and associations. A *Chamber Account* records an

"Item paid to John Heminges . . . dated att Whitehall xx die Maij 1613, for presentinge before the Princes Highnes the Lady Elizabeth and the Prince Pallatyne Elector . . . *The Tempest*."[6]

It is reasonable to suppose, though it cannot be proved, that in Shakespeare's lifetime the King's Men also would have probably presented *The Tempest* with its lyrical songs and poetic passages in the indoor enclosure of the Blackfriars where basic admission was a relatively high sixpence, and perhaps under less favorable conditions in "open air" performance at the Globe, where basic admission was only one pence. But as a matter of historical record, the only early performances known to have been mounted were those before the king and court, the first almost surely staged in the Masquing House, and the second for a royal wedding celebration, probably staged there as well.

This study examines *The Tempest* in critical and historical contexts as a drama, but as a drama having unique masque-like qualities. The study concentrates upon the relatively neglected subject of the known performances of *The Tempest* at Whitehall in 1611 and 1613, and upon the importance of this court background in assessing the wider form and meaning of the play. While attention will be given to scholarship and criticism on the assumed early performances of the drama at Blackfriars or Globe, the *documented* court productions and their milieu will be emphasized in seeking an authoritative "performance text" for the drama; in gauging the possible influence upon Shakespeare, not only of well-known authors and dramatists, but of lesser-known court theatrical writers as well; in analyzing conflicting and intersecting views on the work's genre and structure; in noting the impact of European and English court spectacles and masquing "Triumphs" on the form of the play; and, finally, in interpreting the play's wider symbolism in the light of dramatic conflicts and spectacles of strangeness.

Recently, a number of scholars and critics have again called attention to long-recognized but divergent voyage and New World references in Shakespeare's plays—for example, to island "hurricanoes" in *King Lear*; to the exotic "potato" in *Troilus and Cressida*; to New World mineral wealth in *The Comedy of Errors, The Merchant of Venice*, and *Twelfth Night*; and to Europeans shipwrecked on a strange island in *The Tempest*. Through very wide intertextual discourse, commentators such as Dominique O. Manmoni, Terence Hawkes and Paul Brown seek to identify themes, particularly in *The Tempest*, relating to the Americas and to native populations in both the New World and the old. Under the pressure of modern ideological interest in issues of power, ethnicity and colonial rule, one strain of this criticism has insisted that the play, beyond containing well-known oblique or possible allusions to the New World, is "centered" on the theme of colonialism. This commentary has maintained that Caliban, not Prospero or Miranda or Ferdinand, is the play's central character, a type of the seemingly threatening but actually victimized native "Other" suffering under and rebelling against foreign oppression. Prospero is then seen as symbolic of the harsh European tyrant and slave owner. The magical island then becomes a symbolic reflection of the colonized New World, subject to the territorial and political domination of a foreign noble. In this political-ideological perspective, the play is said to provide a "critique" of European colonialism; and in those readings giving recognition to the author as well as to "intertextualities," Shakespeare, presumed to be somewhat concealing and so "mystifying" his underlying theme out of fear of the censor and an oppressive monarchical establishment, is viewed as an anticolonial political writer.[7]

Alternative readings take exception to the narrow focus of such sharply etched colonial interpretations while still holding the view that Caliban may, to some degree, at least early in the play, mirror stereotypical renderings of New World "ethnic" natives. Other analyses, finding alleged allusions to the colonized New World all or in part "problematic," have retained the popular term "colonial," but have applied it to Prospero's "colonial" family relations or to the literary practice of "colonial linguistics."[8] Moreover, very recent studies examining revisionist colonial commentary in the light of the history of Shakespeare criticism have argued that the body of recent New World and colonial "core" interpretations are overdrawn attempts at political "appropriation," and that Caliban is so original a creation and his role so unique, that this individualized monster cannot be convincingly identified with any colonized native in the New World and elsewhere.[9]

In concentrating upon the court productions and the spectacle and masque-like nature of Shakespeare's drama, the present study maintains that the sweeping and very original socio-political-occultist-religious symbolism of *The Tempest*, in part derived from the novel open symbolism of court writers, can be seen to encompass certain oblique or implied New World and colonial references that in text and subtext give further dimension to the play. The study takes note of the tempestuous sea of political controversy surrounding the drama; and in the last chapter it gives particular attention to the unusual way in which New World natives and themes were actually presented on the Whitehall masquing stage. But the study primarily focuses on advancing an original analysis of genre, structure and symbolism by stressing the special function of the theatrical spectacles of strangeness in giving meaning and form to the entire drama.

The traditional Revels Office involvement in Whitehall productions such as *The Tempest* is in itself revealing. During the 1611–13 period, it was the practice of the Revels Office at St. John's Gate, Clerkenwell—where the scenery, costumes and revels mechanics were accommodated—to take a hand in the rehearsal and "perfection" of court presentations so that they might be suitable for the King and the nobility. As Thomas Heywood states in his *Apology for Actors* published within a year of the first production of *The Tempest*:

> And amongst vs, one of our best *English* Chroniclers records that when *Edward* the fourth would shew himselfe in publicke state to the view of the people, hee repaired to

> the Palace at *S. Johnes*, where he accustomed to see the Citty Actors. And since then, that house by the Princes free gift hath belonged to the office of the Reuels, where our court playes haue beene in late daies yearely rehersed, perfected and corrected before they come to the publike view of the Prince and the Nobility.[10]

Having been rehearsed and perfected under the auspices of the Revels Office, the play's first documented performance in 1611 would then have apparently been in the chamber of the Old Masquing House, which according to accounts of the time was approximately 170 feet long by 50 or 60 feet wide, with a 40-foot quire stage, three feet from the ground.[11] The House had been built in 1518 and then reconstructed in 1606 for the production of masques and theatrical entertainments. In a note dated 6 January 1617/18, Orazio Busino, Almoner to the Venetian Embassy, provided an eyewitness description of the interior. The House, he said,

> is fitted up like a theatre, with well-secured boxes all around. The stage is at one end, and his Majesty's chair under an ample canopy. Near him are stools for the foreign ambassadors. . . . The whole is of wood, including even the shafts, which are carved and gilt with much skill. From the roof of these hang festoons and angels in relief with two rows of light.[12]

The term "boxes" refers to recesses, separated by columns and fitted with seats, along the sides of the walls; Inigo Jones used the word to identify the recesses on his drawings of the stage and Great Hall at Whitehall for the pastoral play *Florimène*.[13] Seating was on *tiers* or *degrees*, wooden planks erected in steps or *gradi*, placed against walls on three sides of the hall. At the rear-center, well away from the walls but facing the raised stage, the king, enthroned under a canopy, was uplifted on a platform to the same height as the stage. Only from the king's throne could the stage settings be viewed in "perfect" perspective. Between the royal seat of state at one narrow end of the hall and the stage, framed by a proscenium arch, at the other was a large, open performing space at the middle of the hall at floor level, a space covered by a huge green carpet. Steps led down from the apron of the stage to this central performing space which generally was used for theatrical compliments to the state and for climactic main masque dances.

Royal celebratory presentations were predominantly staged in the Masquing House and on a few scattered occasions in the rectangular but smaller Great Hall. Between 1605 through 1613, along with plays and other entertainments, eight masques are known to have been mounted in the Banqueting House; three others were staged at court, possibly in the House; and two masques were relegated to the Great Hall, apparently because sequential productions over holiday seasons made it necessary to use another, though smaller, performing site. A still smaller performance chamber, the semicircular Cockpit at Court which had been redesigned from an actual cock pit for informal theatrical presentations, was not used for ceremonial royal productions before the full court.

At the Banqueting House, a court setting quite different from the setting at the Globe or at Blackfriars, *The Tempest* would have posed no special staging or acting difficulties for the members of Shakespeare's company. As a professional group, the company appears to have been flexible, able to present different genres of dramas in different ways to different audiences under different staging conditions. When the Chamberlain's men were officially appointed as the King's actors on 19 May 1603, their appointment papers specified that they would perform in what was obviously intended as an inclusive range of staged works: "Comedies, tragedies, histories, Enterludes, Morralles, Pastoralls, Stageplayes, and suche like."[14] They would also have been expected to appear in masques in the roles of disruptive or virtuous supporting figures especially during festival seasons when plays and masques were staged on alternate nights. But as commoners, they would not have been given main roles. Samuel Daniel notes an exception to the use of commoners as masque supporting performers, and so confirms its general practice, in the stage directions to *Tethys Festival: or The Queenes wake* (1610), a work mounted at court just eight months before the initial production of *The Tempest*: "... there were none of the inferiour sort," he comments archly, "mixed amongst these great Personages of State and Honour (as usually there haue beene)."[15]

From long experience, Shakespeare and the other members of the King's Men would have had a thorough knowledge of court stagecraft, including that stagecraft featuring Inigo Jones's lavish changeable scenery and ingenious stage machines. From the time of King James's accession to the throne in 1603 until the year of the first Whitehall performance of *The Tempest* in 1611, the King's Men had performed every year at court in an average of between 13 and 14 recorded productions, and they very often appeared during holiday Revels periods when plays, interspersed with masques, were presented on consecutive evenings. On two occasions, James's delight in theatricals even overcame his fear of infection from the plague. When this scourge raged in London in 1603–04 and again in 1608–09, additional payments were made to the King's Men for braving contagion and acting at court. Year by year, the number of their court performances increased. In 1603–04, eight plays were recorded as being produced before the royal presence. During the season of 1610–11, the number had risen to 15; and by 1611/12, to 22 including *The Tempest*.[16]

Given this theatrical background and the political and social situation at the time, Shakespeare could very possibly have composed *The Tempest* in late 1610 and in 1611, introducing visionary spectacles and a visionary betrothal masque in anticipation of a likely staging of the work in the Masquing House at a royal betrothal or wedding celebration.

For some 12 months before the performance of the play at Whitehall on 1 November 1611, reports circulated in the English court of the impending betrothal of the King's daughter Princess Elizabeth to a prospective ruler, most probably to the King's constant favorite, Protestant Frederick V of

Palatine, rather than to the Spanish Catholic candidate at times favored by Queen Anne. According to a dispatch by Venetian ambassador Marc Antonio Correr at the English court dated 2 September 1610, "their majesties" were said to be "inclined to no one so much as to the Prince Palatine," although the ambassador noted later in the month that the Queen now leaned toward a Spanish alliance.[17] On 24 February 1611, the Venetian ambassador reported that Frederick, instead of sending a representative to negotiate the marriage, was "coming in person" (181).

In March the ambassador noted that the king is "greatly inclined to the match" and that the Elector will be "coming himself in a few months" (202). On 21 April 1611 the ambassador observed that Frederick had instead decided to send an envoy to "ask for the Princess in the Palatine's name" (204), but in July the ambassador changes this story again to state that Frederick will come himself (207). In September of 1611, Frederick instead attended a Diet of Protestant Princes, convened by the occultist Holy Roman Emperor Rudolf II in Rothenberg to counter the European Catholic League. Then on 28 October 1611 the Diet sent an envoy to James asking that he formally agree to the marriage of Elizabeth and Frederick and that the king give the Protestant Princes his political and military support.[18]

King James, though an avowed enemy of magicians, agreed to the Protestant bridegroom who was the son of an occultist; and in November of 1611, the month of the first recorded performance of *The Tempest*, the king announced the engagement of the Princess to Frederick. The wedding and its celebration took place on 14 November 1613, the year of the play's second performance at Whitehall.

Fifty-six years after the second court production, John Dryden, in a preface dated "Decemb. 1. 1669," which introduced the printed version of his and William Davenant's Shakespearean musical adaptation *The Tempest or the Enchanted Island* (1670), observed in passing that Shakespeare's drama "had formerly been acted with success in the Black-Fryers."[19] Commentary and notes for editions of

The Tempest sometimes record this comment, but without always adding that Dryden was probably referring to performances that took place during the Restoration. Shakespeare had long been dead, and public theatrical tastes in the intervening period had inclined toward musical "heroic dramas" with modest spectacle and scenic settings. When Dryden made his remark, the Blackfriars had long abandoned the practice, followed in Shakespeare's period, of staging dramas without backflat scenery or notable properties. The theatre during the Restoration instead mounted plays using what J. Isaacs calls "the masque technique" which, though much less elaborate than Inigo Jones's massive court productions, nevertheless included a "full scenic stage," "extensive properties," and considerable music and dance.[20] Seats at Blackfriars were placed in rows throughout the hall proper and around the uplifted stage at the far end, and a new Restoration verisimilitude governed these later Blackfriars' productions. Significantly, the text and stage directions of the new work suggest that Dryden and former masque writer Davenant clearly recognized in Shakespeare's play those special spectacle elements drawn from the masque, elements adaptable to Restoration heroic dramas staged with scenery and featuring exotic locales and characters.

Even a cursory examination of *The Tempest* discloses that—unlike most of the early or late history plays, comedies, tragedies and so-called final romances that are set over extended periods in different indoor and outdoor locales—this drama takes place, like court spectacles, in the approximate time needed for performance; and it unfolds within a masque-like iconographic cosmos of the sort Inigo Jones depicted in his court stage designs and carried over from masque to masque. The neorealist settings of Shakespeare's earlier dramas—chambers in court, closets, towns, castles, battlefields—here give way to a familiar, centralized, iconographic locale: the cell of the magician Prospero on an island of enchantments. Action begins with a sudden, noisy tempest-at-sea spectacle and then as suddenly changes to the apparent quiet of the cell where the aged Prospero "instructs" his daughter Miranda, a youthful figure who finally dozes under the spell of her father's magic. The action then shifts to other parts of the island where characters wander as in a "maze" until they fall into an enchanted sleep. All action occurs, as the text makes clear, in a moving masque-like iconographic cosmos composed of the elements of earth, air, fire and water and subject to the movements of the seasons, storms, tides and heavens. In one visionary spectacle, Prospero stands "at the top" as did controlling figures in Whitehall scenic representations. In another, Ariel enters, perhaps seemingly floating through the air, disguised as a Harpy and wearing the wings regularly donned by theatrical "airy" character-types. And in a masque within the play, the goddess Juno "descends," as the Folio stage directions record, in what at Whitehall would have been the traditional masque-like levitation of this conventional masque figure from the heavens to the stage.

And if the play appears to contain more in the way of spectacle than other works by Shakespeare, it contains less in the way of plot. Through Prospero's magic, plans by aristocrats Stephano and Antonio—and parallel plans by Caliban, Trinculo and Stephano—to gain political power by murder are thwarted. And through Prospero's magic, Miranda and Ferdinand are kept together at the Magus's cell until they are betrothed. Then Prospero stages a series of magical "entries" and "discoveries" that reveal the underlying true identities of the main characters and, largely through awe and wonder, stimulate changes in their feelings and thoughts that result in reconciliations.

"There is really not very much plot in *The Tempest*," Hallett Smith comments, expressing a widely held critical opinion. "There are situations, spectacle, music, contrasts of character, and rich poetry"; and these, as Smith points out, make us "overlook the fact that there is no significant dramatic struggle and that actually very little happens."[21]

And like no other drama by Shakespeare, the play is unique in capturing a sense of the evanescence of mortal life that was a central experience of court masques: the sense that the joys of human existence are like an ephemeral dream that quickly fades and is forever gone. This nostalgic *carpe diem* experience is repeatedly emphasized by the fact that the word "now"—carrying in context the implication that what is immediate will momentarily pass away—appears approximately twice as many times in this short play, as recorded in concordances than it does in other plays in the canon.[22] Prospero's poignant "fabric-of-a-vision" speech, with its actual reminiscences of scenes that had appeared on the Whitehall stage, echoes the nostalgic comments of Ben Jonson on the passing away of the wondrous "apparelling" of his masque *Hymenaei*:

> Such was the exquisit performance, as (beside the *pompe, splendor*, or what we may call *apparelling* of such *Presentments*) that alone (had all else beene absent) was of power to surprize with delight, and steale away the *spectators* from themselues. Nor was there wanting whatsoeuer might giue to the *furniture*, or *complement*; eyther in *riches* or strangenesse of the *habites*, delicacie of *daunces*, magnificence of the *scene*, or diuine rapture of *musique*. Onely the enuie was, that it lasted not still, or (now it is past) cannot by imagination, much lesse description, be recouered to a part of that *spirit* it had in the gliding by.[23]

Ultimately, although surviving documents allow for only a restricted knowledge of the circumstances surrounding the composition of *The Tempest*, the available evidence suggests that this play about a magician who controls apparitions and an airy spirit—a play that was first presented at Whitehall on "Hallomas nyght" and that includes a betrothal masque—could have been written, not only for possible private and public theatre staging, but especially for staging at court before King James during a particular season of the year for the particular occasion of an anticipated betrothal or wedding celebration. And as David Bergeron has suggested, the play with its themes of thwarted sedition, reconciliation, and joyful, imminent royal family marriage could well have been written to embrace in a vague and very general way political concerns that so absorbed the English court in the 1611–13 period: namely, concerns about the potential for political sedition, about the arrangement of political alliances through marriage, and about heirs to succeed to the English throne.[24]

Examinations of the actual staging practices at Whitehall; of the Revels Office Rolls for 1603–38 in the British Records Office; of staging and theatrical allusions in the 1623 Folio text of the drama; of neglected "new" theories by court writers on imaginative theatrical invention; of "old" theories and practices arising from classical Latin play structures and conventions; of early *intermezzo*, late Jonsonian and other masquing Triumphs; of a host of early pastoral, tragic-comic and "romance" theatrical and literary works; of the European court spectacles serving as background to English and Shakespearean theatrical works; and of a wide range of recent complementary and conflicting scholarly and critical assessments—all of these studies point to *The Tempest* as a unique transitional drama with an original structure, a drama fashioned for presentation as needed at public and private theatres, but written primarily for the special machines and conditions of the stage at Whitehall.

My contention is that the Folio text reveals a highly imaginative sensitivity to court staging potential, and that certain values and subtleties of the play's possible early presentation can be grasped, not by emending the stage directions in the Folio to accommodate assumed but undocumented Blackfriars or Globe presentations in Shakespeare's lifetime, but by reexamining how staging references might have been realized in the known 1611 and 1613 court productions.

Following an opening chapter that explores differing interpretations of the play's genre and structure, *The Tempest* is analyzed in the second chapter as an amalgam of Renaissance forms in transition, a play having a unique structure strongly influenced by the international *intermezzo* ballet and the English masque. The staging of *The Tempest* at

Whitehall is then examined in the next chapter in the light of overlooked stage practices at court and allusions in the 1623 Folio text. In approaching the elusive symbolism of the play, chapter 4 investigates the neglected revisionist views of court writers favoring original inventions and imaginative iconography largely free of neoclassical meaning and convention. A final chapter focuses on the play as a symbolic spectacle of wonder in which fanciful dreams of a Golden Age are shattered by a gradual recognition of an actual social world that is mortal and limiting.

The Tempest, this study maintains, responded to a fascination at court with staged spectacles that embraced all of the theatrical arts—song, speech, scenery, dance and costume iconography—and that featured strange or unusual character-types in exotic locales. And it anticipated audience fascination later in the century with comparable theatrical works, with similarly exotic settings, cast in the new forms of the Restoration heroic drama. The play thus points forward in its theatrical outlook more than it points back. For although the new verisimilitude of the Restoration stage emphasized stylization at the expense of dramatic force, Shakespeare's play, with its masque-like qualities, survived in popular though often dramatically diminished versions, not only in Davenant's and Dryden's *The Tempest, or the Enchanted Island* (1670), but also in the "operatic" revision of uncertain authorship under the same title (1674); in the farcical version by Thomas Duffett *The Mock-Tempest: or The Enchanted Castle* (1675); in the Garrick musical version *The Tempest, An Opera* (1756) which proved a failure; and finally in a production of the original play under the original title (1757), which was acclaimed as a theatrical success.[25]

ONE

Theatrical Forms in Transition

In a brief reference to *The Tempest* in his study of the genre and form of Shakespeare's major and minor plays, T. W. Baldwin in *Shakespeare's Five Act Structure* states of the playwright that "his first surviving play, *Love's Labor's Lost* is the most original in structure of all his plays, unless it be his last, *The Tempest*."[1] Having exhaustively examined the teaching in English Latin grammar schools of the academic Latin play form, especially that of the Roman dramatist Publius Terence; Baldwin registered the strong impact of that academic form on Shakespeare and other English playwrights. But Baldwin's remark on *The Tempest* remains enigmatic, for he does not offer any clear analysis of Shakespeare's play showing what its "most original structure" might be.

Baldwin's omission is understandable. Interpretations of and theories about the genre and structure of *The Tempest* are so varied, and the conclusions reached so often conflicting, that it might at first appear that this "problem play" survives despite its critics. Yet this disparity of views points to something very fundamental in the nature of the work: its singularity as a drama composed by a working playwright seemingly aware of but not bound by contemporaneous theatrical conventions. R. A. Foakes is surely correct in asserting that "*The Tempest* has its own distinctive structure, sets up its own peculiar pattern of expectations, and demands to be assessed as a unique work of art in its own right."[2]

Before attempting such an assessment in later chapters, critical perspective can be gained by examining varying claims about the work advanced in past and recent years. Does *The Tempest* have the essential form of an epic romance, or a classical Terentian drama, or a pastoral tragecomedy, or a Jonsonian masque of types and antitypes, or a novel "inverted" masque of types, or some combination of these or other theatrical structural patterns? In looking into these structural matters, it is helpful to begin by considering how the play was "set out" and labeled when initially printed in the Folio edition of 1623.

No designation of genre appears on title page one of this opening work in the Folio collection, or elsewhere on the printed pages of the drama. But a frontispiece "Catalogve" of all the plays in the Folio—one possibly prepared by John Heminge and Henrie Condell or by the scrivener Ralph Crane—lists *The Tempest* first under the heading "Comedies" in a column of 14 works that includes just one other of the "last" plays: *The Winter's Tale*. Another late play, *Cymbeline*, is placed at the end of a column of six dramas under the heading "Tragedies," and the late play Pericles is not listed or otherwise included at all, a fact contributing to speculation through the centuries that the drama was of mixed authorship.

Because all of the plays cited as "Comedies" have plots

concluding with reconciliations, they are loosely and inconclusively categorized following typical Renaissance norms of the sort stated in 1612 by Thomas Heywood in *An Apology for Actors* (1612): "Comedies begin in trouble and end in peace; Tragedies begin in calme, and end in tempest."[3] Shakespeare, in seeking a sweeping symbolic theme for his play had only to toy archly with such definitions, creating a "comedy" beginning with "tempest" and ending in peace.

In a prefatory statement *To the great Variety of Readers* opening the 1623 Folio, John Heminge and Henrie Condell write that the texts of the plays, said to have been previously "maimed, and deformed by the frauds and stealthes of iniurious impostors," have now been "cur'd" and made "perfect of their limbes"—comments suggesting that hands other than dead Shakespeare's edited the plays and divided at least some of their presumed "limbes" into acts and scenes in accord with the supposed "perfect" form of Latin plays (D. A3). Those dramas earlier printed in quarto had lacked such divisions. The very probable late insertion of "perfect" Latin act divisions into the dramas is suggested by the fact that, in the 1623 Folio, act "headings" appear printed in the text, not in English, but in Latin.

The view that act and scene divisions are a late interpolation receives support from the haphazard way in which the divisions are introduced into the plays. Act and scene divisions are entirely missing—with the exception of the opening page designation "*Actus Primus, Scoena Prima*"—from the following plays as they appear in the Folio (in this order and with this pagination): *Histories: The Second Part of Henry the Sixt, with the death of the Good Duke Hvmfrey*, D. 120–146; *The third Part of Henry the Sixt, with the death of the Duke of Yorke*, D. 147–172; *Tragedies: The Tragedie of Troylus and Creside*, D. 77 and ff. unnumbered pages; *The Tragedie of Romeo and Ivliet*, D. 53–79; *The Life of Tymon of Athens*, D. 80–99; *The Tragedie of Anthonie, and Cleopatra*, D. 340–368. A curious feature of the Folio is that *The Life of Henry the Fift*, D. 69–95; which has the usual

Actus Primus, Scoena Prima on the first page of dialogue, is divided into a total of five acts with no scenes within them. *The Tragedie of Hamlet*, D. 152–280, is divided into two opening acts with scene divisions, but with no other later scene or act divisions.[4]

Thus, critics trying to uncover the form and multiple genre derivations of *The Tempest*, aware that the work was perhaps not initially written in acts, have understandably been both stimulated and troubled by the theatrical eclecticism of Shakespeare and his playwright contemporaries. In Italy and France, sixteenth century members of the academies, in the manner of contemporary theorists, scrupulously struggled to define "mixed-genre" dramas with slight concern for theoretical and literary tradition, but with an eye to the occasion, the political and religious climate, the censor, and both courtly and public audiences. English writers whose works were presented at court, particularly those composing commissioned entertainments and masques, were especially under the domination of the occasion and their aristocratic or royal patrons. "All these courtly, and honouring inventions . . .," George Chapman writes in an "answer" to "objections" in introducing the *Masque of the Middle Temple*, ". . . should expressuely arise out of the places, and persons, for and by whom they are presented."[5]

Commentators have used the vague category of "romance" to denote diverse Renaissance plays with tragic, comic and miraculous elements, but especially to signify in Shakespeare's late plays *Pericles, Cymbeline, The Winter's Tale* and *The Tempest* serious but nonrealistic modes of representation usually characteristic of the category. "Romance," a name derived from the Medieval Latin word *romanice* and the Old French word *roman*, has come to be applied through the ages to works having an all but indefinable mixture of love interests, marvelous or magical occurrences, adventurous quests, religious or occultist themes, and pastoral episodes. Medieval and early Renaissance works considered as romances have tended to center upon legends about Arthur, Charlemagne, Christian saints, and ancient heroes such as Aeneas, Jason and Alexander, with historical or semihistorical stories about crusaders and Saracens included as well. *The Tempest* has been placed in the tradition of the somewhat different but still recognizable Renaissance romance because of its stress upon the magical and the marvelous, its strong pastoral and occultist elements, its references to adventurous and tempestuous voyage, and its concentration upon "love interests" associated with events in early heroic works. As discussed in chapter 5, passages in *The Tempest* allude to a relationship between the hero Jason and the witch Medea of a kind recounted in romance episodes of Apollonius Rhodius' epic *Argonautica* and Ovid's *Metamorphoses*. The play also alludes to the "love interest" of Dido for Aeneas as it appears in Virgil's *Aeneid*.

Critics have drawn distant parallels between *The Tempest* and European and English romance dramas of the Renaissance, such as Giovanni Battista Guarini's play *Il Pastor Fido* (1585) and Samuel Daniel's "Pastoral Trage-Comedie" *The Queen's Arcadia* (1605), with aristocratic character-types acting out love relationships in pastoral settings. The most arresting of these background works is the crude, diffuse, anonymously written English play *Mucedorus* (1589), published without acts and revived by the King's Men about 1610, depicting royal and aristocratic lovers in woodland scenes, a wild man Bremo, and the allegorical figures Comedie and Envie who debate whether this comedy should become a tragedy.[6] Predictably, romance-pastoral source materials have been extended to include general dramatic episodes and emblematic types from early books of Spenser's *The Faerie Queene*, most notably book 3.

In one instance, an early critic, Colin Still, interpreted presumed cyclical pastoral components in *The Tempest* as allegorical, and as evidence that the drama is basically a neo-Platonic mystery play that mirrors rites of initiation and rebirth originally acted out at Eleusis between about 1000 B.C. to 300 A.D. According to Still, the allegory is said to concern Ceres' journey into the underworld to return her daughter Persephone, a captive of Pluto, to the surface world. Miranda, then, represents Persephone; Ferdinand, the male god of the Eleusian mysteries; Prospero, the hierophant controlling the ceremonies; and the "three Men of Sin," corrupt mortals on a journey to the underworld that results in their spiritual rebirth.[7]

Though properly stressing themes of sin, distraction and regeneration, this interpretation—which has been sharply criticized over the years—superimposes an overly restrictive pattern of ideological meanings upon suggestive, but far from specific, "open" symbolism, a symbolism that will be seen to reflect the new views of seventeenth century modernist theatrical writers. In addition, neither Still nor other commentators have been able to demonstrate convincingly, either from Shakespeare's early work or from outside sources, that the playwright knew about or even had access to mystery play sources. Recognizing these problems, Michael Srigley has recently offered an alternative allegorical reading that stresses regeneration, with Prospero interpreted as an alchemist in need of logs to fire his experiments. The "men of sin" are said to be alchemically and spiritually reborn after immersion in a catalyst of salt sea water, and after the "distraction" caused by the antic visionary spectacles. Their rebirth is found to take place under the auspices of Ferdinand and Miranda, the presumed restorative alchemical king and queen who will introduce a Golden Age.[8]

The Tempest does appear to contain a number of actual or possible alchemical references, for example, Prospero's "Proiect" (D. 16), might allude to alchemical projection; the Magus's comment on how the men of sin's brains "boile" (D. 16), to alchemical treatises on the skull as a receptacle in which to boil substances. But such scattered and oblique alchemical allusions, cast within the matrix of rich and enigmatic passages invoking wider occult powers associated with episodes in classical literature are too slight a textual base upon which to erect a comprehensive allegorical-ideological reading. Shakespeare's play reflects in its magical lore, symbolically rather than allegorically, only some possible alchemical allusions of the kind used by John Donne in his early poetry and *The First Anniversarie* (1611), and harshly mocked by Ben Jonson in his play *The Alchemist* (1610) and his masque *Mercurie Vindicated from the Alchemist at Court* (1615).

There is no need to go back to arcane alchemical sources or to the Elusian mysteries to find works that might have immediately inspired Shakespeare's themes and references. In 1606 Ben Jonson celebrated the renewal of life through wedded union in the masque *Hymenaei,* a work presented in part before a stage "Altar" as a theatrical religious "rite" or "ceremony" and including as character-types the goddesses Iris and Juno. Musicians moving in procession to the Altar establish the masque's theme in an opening song:

> Bid all profane away;
> None here may stay
> To view our *mysteries,*
> But, who themselues haue beene,
> Or will, in time, be seene
> The self-same *sacrifice.*
> For Vnion, *Mistris* of these *rites*
> Will be obseru'd with eyes,
> As simple as her nights.[9]

A final *Epithalamium,* sung to a bride and groom in a concluding procession, highlights the topos of renewal.

> So may they both, e're day,
> Rise perfect euerie way.
> And, when the *babe* to light is showne,
> Let it be like each *parent* knowne;
> Much of the *fathers* face,
> More of the *mothers* grace
>
> (7.228, ll. 547–52)

Pageant plays about the gods, such as the *The Rare Triumphs of Loue and Fortune* (1589) and plays in the *commedia dell'arte* tradition, have been added to romance and allegorical drama as possible influences upon Shakespeare.[10] However, these pageant and *commedia* influences—because they lack detailed analogues in plot, characters, settings and themes with *The Tempest*—remain very general.

Historically, *The Tempest* has long been read against the background of contemporaneous romance-style accounts of the much-discussed wreck of the British ship *Sea Adventure* in the Bermudas in July 1609. Tracts published or circulated during the following months recounted how the ship, which was carrying colonists under Sir Thomas Gates and Sir George Summers to Virginia, had run aground on rocks off a luxuriant island, and how all aboard had safely gained the land, where they lived on rescued ship's supplies but also on the delicious and abundant local produce. In May of 1610, Gates, Summers and the company set out again for Virginia and finally reached their destination. Among the works that told of the storm, the wreck and the extraordinary island were William Strachey's letter, the *True Reportory of the Wrack of July 1610*, published in *Purchas His Pilgrimes* (1625); Sylvester Jourdain's *Discovery of the Barmudas* (1610), and the Council of Virginia's *True Declaration of the state of the Colonie in Virginia, with a confutation of such scandalous reports as have tended to the discrace of so worthy an enterprise* (1610). In addition, related travel publications such as Richard Hakluyt's *Principall Navigations, Voiages and Discoveries of the English nation* (1583, and later editions)—together with medieval and Renaissance literature on wild men, savages and strange races—including the fictional monsters of *The Book of Sir John Maundeville* and of Montaigne's essay on the noble cannibals—have been rightly cited as providing an exotic mixture of materials vaguely reflected in Shakespeare's theatrical enchanted island and its inhabitants.

Within the play, too, are specific colonial themes that appear to arise from voyage tracts and books recording Spanish brutality against New World natives. These themes, modified but recognizable, are evident in Prospero's caustic treatment and "enslavement" of the "native" Caliban.

They reverberate too when foreign seamen give liquor to Caliban and the monster becomes drunk; when Caliban pathetically adores these corrupting foreigners as gods; when Prospero dominates the unlettered monster through art; and when this natural "savage" rebels by attempting to violate Prospero's daughter, and by plotting Prospero's murder.

But Shakespeare, who could have set his play in the colonial New World, chose instead to locate action on a magical Mediterranean island, and so, at a stroke, self-consciously established and developed a context that gives the drama dimensions of meaning that both include and subsume the colonial. One strain of what seems to me reductionist political interpretation, advanced without accompanying genre or structural analysis, insists through theoretical readings that New World colonial material constitutes the very "center" of the play, and that Caliban is the play's hero and central figure.

In one critical variant, interpreters have sought universal psychic patterns of colonialist tyranny in the drama, reflective of the actual historical and psychic situations of colonized native populations. Dominique O. Manmoni, in a literalist but wide-ranging psychological reading, maintains that Caliban has Madagascan-African character traits and, as such, serves as a psychic type for persons everywhere suffering from colonialist oppression. Sibnarayn Ray associates the experiences and subjugation of Caliban with those of repressed peoples under apartheid, while Edward Kamau Brathwaite finds Caliban's rebellion against Prospero comparable to the rebellion of Jamaican slaves against French colonialists.[11]

In another variant, commentators have isolated selected passages and read them using modernist, postmodernist and linguistic-analytical techniques in the search for hidden or suppressed, but supposedly "core," anticolonialist content. Barbadian novelist George Lamming fostered a strain of "linguistic colonial" criticism, later elaborated by Terence Hawkes and Stephen Greenblatt, in claiming that, because

Caliban states that he learned a language from Prospero, the creature can be seen as confined to the Magus's linguistic prison and so culturally colonized and oppressed.[12] Hawkes, by means of an imaginative but, I think, misleading extended metaphor, maintained that Shakespeare, too, is a colonialist.[13] Commenting on Shakespeare and other playwrights, Hawkes writes that "the dramatist is metaphorically a colonist" when he aggressively "penetrates new areas of experience," egocentrically "makes new territory over in his own image," and engages in "raids on the articulate" with the aim of opening "new worlds for the imagination" (212). If accepted, this metaphor allows nearly any imaginative episode in *The Tempest* to be labeled a colonialist appropriation. Moreover, the dramatist Shakespeare becomes a nonmimetic, modernist writer, shaping plays in his own personal image, and engaging in colonial raids and penetrations, the last having possible erotic overtones, simply by imaginatively practicing his art.

After approvingly quoting Hawke's dramatist-colonist metaphor, and also Hawke's unconvincing assertion that "Shakespeare's imagination was fired by the resemblance he perceived between himself and a colonist" (p. 24), Stephen Greenblatt advances this dramatist-colonist association as an accepted axiom of criticism.[14] "The problem for critics," Greenblatt writes, "has been to accommodate this perceived resemblance between dramatist and colonist with a revulsion that reaches from the political critiques of colonialism in our own century back to the moral outrage of Las Casas and Montaigne" (24). Reading brief passages of *The Tempest* without full regard for contexts, Greenblatt, based on the fallacious assumption that dramatists resemble colonists, discerns in the play a clear episode of "linguistic colonialism," one upon which he bases the title of his book. After Caliban states in act 1 that Prospero taught him to name the bigger and lesser lights in the sky, and after Prospero adds that he also taught Caliban the names of the hours, Caliban—who at this juncture is accused by Prospero of having attempted the rape of Miranda and is derided as a "slave"—angrily responds that his "profit" on learning language from the Magus is that he knows "how to curse." Because the actions and speech of the brutish Caliban here suggest that he did indeed attempt the rape, and because the Magus does not fit the overall pattern of the traditional colonist, this situation, I think, cannot be judged in terms of unqualified moral absolutes favoring Caliban, even when the shaping power of language is acknowledged. Yet Greenblatt, perceiving Caliban as the wronged victim of "linguistic colonialism," insists that "we" experience from Caliban's lines "a sense of their devastating justness. Ugly, rude, savage, Caliban nevertheless achieves for an instant an absolute if intolerably bitter moral victory. There is no reply: only Prospero's command: 'Hagseed, hence!/Fetch us fuel,' coupled with an ugly threat" (24). "Our" supposed reactions are thus forced into accord with Greenblatt's theory of linguistic victimization.

Other critics such as Bruce Erlich and Paul N. Siegal have turned to linguistic codes or ironies in seeking to uncover central colonialist content.[15] Yet as a detailed structural analysis and a contextual reading of the entire play and its "open" symbolism will suggest, the actual or possible colonial allusions appear, not at any insisted upon "center," but as part of the play's wider antic and ordering symbolism and action.

The play's action, as we have stressed, takes place on an island in the Meditteranean rather than in the New World; the island "natives" turn out to be a subhuman monster and an airy spirit. The magician Prospero, who temporarily rules the monster and spirit, has arrived on the island not by design on a colonial expedition, but by chance after having been deposed as Duke of Milan and having been set adrift by enemies in a small boat. This magician-ruler, unlike Caliban, does not desire land and makes no territorial claims. After magically confounding his aristocratic enemies and arranging a reconciliation with them, he decides to leave permanently and to return to Milan. At the end of the play, he sets the airy spirit free and surrenders future control of the Mediterranean island to the monster. In short, the drama's setting, characters, action and overriding general symbolism hardly fit the usual pattern of European colonialism.

Differing from colonial interpretations, other recent readings offer genre and structural analysis based on the "romance epic" tradition. In the most elaborate, Donna B. Hamilton argues that *The Tempest* in form and adjusted narrative imitates the first six books of Virgil's *Aeneid*. The seemingly lustful passion of Dido for Aeneas, Hamilton claims, is reversed and "repossessed" in the chaste love of Ferdinand and Miranda, and Aeneas's visit to the underworld is recapitulated in the play's visionary masque-like interludes. Virgilian epic representations of storm and wandering, she argues, are mirrored in the drama's encompassing themes and action.[16]

Hamilton—citing wide reference in the play to Dido, Carthage and classical goddesses—plausibly interprets the betrothal masque of chaste love as Shakespeare's reworking and reversal of "the central aspect of Virgil's story" involving the "behavior of Dido and Aeneas on that fateful day when they satisfy their lust in the cave to which they are driven by Juno's storm" (79). Yet her theories about Shakespeare's "concealment" of the play's allegedly underlying epic structure are pressed so far, without adequate supporting analysis, that at times they appear to be modern associative superimpositions. All "conspiracy plots in the play," for example, are said to "depend on the central structural features of that fateful night when the Greeks defeated the Trojans by creeping out of the wooden horse and opening the gates to more Greek soldiers" (16). The "*glistering apparell*" episode involving Caliban, Stephano and Trinculo (D. 15) is, in a strained reading, alleged to be placed so as to be an analogue for that "section of the *Aeneid* where Aeneas finds the golden bough and enters the cave that leads to Pluto's domain" (88).

Certainly, references to Carthage, together with six allusions to Dido or Dido's widow in scene 3 (D. 6–9); the appearance of Ariel like a harpy comparable to the one in the *Aeneid*;[17] and the emphasis on themes of storm, chaste and lustful love, and wandering indeed reflect motifs in Virgil's epic. Further, the play obviously draws upon the symbolism and themes of storm, wandering, harpies, sedition and magic found in the epic-romance tradition, especially in Homer's *Odyssey* and Ovid's *Metamorphosis*. Still, given the play's lyricism, its apparent dramatic unity of time, place and action, and its reliance on stage spectacle, there has always been an understandable critical reluctance about insisting that *The Tempest* owes its deepest forms and meanings to lengthy heroic epics of 12 books or more, epics having conventions and structures in many ways incongruous with those of Renaissance dramas.

Hamilton's selective explication, essentially thematic rather than structural, usefully discloses the Virgilian epic background of a number of key passages in *The Tempest*. But her claim that the play has an epic form is ultimately unconvincing.[18]

In considering how epic romance motifs came to appear in a Shakespearean masque-like drama at court, it should be recalled that classical epic symbols and themes were especially popular in aristocratic staged spectacles, ranging from the French *Balet Comique de la Royne* (1581) featuring Circe, to a multitude of continental court ballets and spectacles centered on classical epic themes culminating in the lavish French *Ballet des Argonautes* (1619), to English masquing Triumphs such as *Proteus and the Adamantine Rock* (1594) with its Homeric character-types, William Browne's *The Inner Temple Masque* (1615) about Circe and Ulysses, and Milton's *A Mask Presented at Ludlow Castle* (1634) about the son of Circe.[19] Homeric, Virgilian and Ovidian figures had wide currency as well in masques by Jonson, Davenant, Thomas Carew, Aurelian Townshend and others; indeed theorists of the sixteenth century European academies conceived of the court masques and the related *balet de cour* as recreations of ancient Greek drama.[20] Modern commentators have found the spectacles to have possible origins in Greek satyr and mystery plays, and to have been influenced by the entries of generals into imperial Rome in staged Triumphs. It was the pervasiveness of epic and classical elements in masques and court spectacles that caused reformers like Samuel Daniel to seek alternative "hieroglyphics" and themes.

In composing a play to be performed before King James, Shakespeare had only to turn for classical "epic" materials to spectacles staged at the Masquing House in the presence of the monarch, and particularly to a work regularly remarked upon by commentators: Ben Jonson's *The Masque of Queenes* (1609). Jonson's text and notes cleverly intermingle epic romance tradition with magic, witchcraft and necromancy; the masque was obviously designed in the manner of Shakespeare's *Macbeth* to appeal to the king's supposed expert knowledge of magic and witchcraft, a knowledge displayed in the monarch's esoteric published work *Daemonologie, in the forme of a Dialogue* (1597).[21] In a prominent note appended to the first printed text of Jonson's masque, the author writes, "See the *Kings Ma.ties* book (or *Soueraigne*) of *Daemonologie*" (7.283, ll. 30–33). Jonson thus called attention to presumed royal learning even as he apparently insured royal approbation and patronage. The masque drew as well upon a widespread aristocratic and popular fascination with magic that had earlier contributed to the theatrical success of Christopher Marlowe's play *The Tragicall History of the Life and Death of Doctor Faustus* (1598), first published in quarto in 1604.

The disorderly antic masquers in Jonson's work, witches with occult powers, seek by magic, in the words of their "Chiefe Dame," to stir up a "Storme" (ll. 285) and by so doing to "make Nature fight/Within her selfe; loose the whole hinge of Things" (ll. 147–48). These denizens of the underworld enter out of a flaming semicircular scenic Hell's mouth at the rear-center of the stage, and each is said to signify the "morall person of a Fury" (ll. 217). Their magical power, according to Jonson's extended explanation of classical sources in the printed text, is that attributed by "*Homer* to *Circe*, in the *Odyss.*," by "*Ouid* . . . to *Medea*, &

Circe, in *Metamorp,*" and by "Virgil to *Alphesiboeus* in his. [Aeneid]" (ll. 209–13). Later, Jonson compares the honor of the main masque figure Camilia to that of Aeneas in book 7 of the *Aeneid* (ll. 495–500).

In his notes to this masque of magical transformations, Jonson emphasizes the extraordinary magical powers of Medea, citing on three occasions (ll. 75–83, 183–86, 217–241) passages on the sorceress and her magic from book 7 of Ovid's *Metamorphosis.*[22] Then Jonson gives the head witch, the "Dam," a ringing rhetorical monologue that paraphrases Medea's declaration on the power of magic in *Metamorphosis* (7.197–219). Jonson's version of the speech contains an apparent "cue" for a Whitehall stage effect: the "darkening" of the stage to the "roof" by lowering canisters, open at both ends, over the "blazing tapers" of candles or oil lamps.

> You Fiendes and Furies, (if yet any bee
> Worse then or selues) You, that haue quak'd, to see
> These knotts vntied; and shrunke, when we haue charm'd.
> . . . .
> . . . When the boystrous Sea,
> Wthout breath of Wind, hath knocked the skie;
> And that hath thundred, *Ioue* no knowing, Why:
> When we haue set the Elements at warres;
> Made Mid-night see the Sunne; and Day the starres;
> When wing'd Lightning, in the course hath stayd;
> And swiftest Riuers haue runne back, afrayd
> To see the Corne remoue, the Groues to range,
> Whole Places alter, and the Seasons change.
> When the pale *Moone,* at the first voyce downe fell
> Poyson'd, and durst not stay the second Spell.
> You that haue, oft, bene conscious of these sights;
> And thou, *three-formed Starre,* that on these nights
> Art only power-full, to Whose tripel Name
> Thus wee incline; *Once, twise,* and *thrise-the-Same*:
> If, now, wth *rites* profane and foule inough,
> Wee doe invoke thee; Darken all this roofe,
> Wth present fogges. Exhale Earths rott'nest vapors;
> And strike a blindnesse, through these blazing tapers.
> (ll. 218–43)

Notably, as commentators have observed, Shakespeare in *The Tempest* also hinges Prospero's climactic power-of-magic speech, just before the Magus's "unmasking," on a paraphrase of words and lines in both the Dam's declaration and in the source passage in the *Metamorphosis*.[23] The declaration by the Magus, in which he speaks of having "bedimmed" the noonday light of the sun, would have been presented, of course, on "Hollowmas nyght" in 1606 before a king who displayed both belief and interest in magicians and witches.

In Jonson's masque, the "Dam" and the other witches, signifying Furies, are "antic" figures who blasphemously invoke and invert Trinitarian numerology, dance "in reverse," and wish to conjure up a genuinely destructive storm. Shakespeare's Prospero, essentially the opposite of an "antic" type, moves normally and never backward, conjures up a "harmless" tempest, overcomes his fury, and "abjures" his occult powers. He is created, in part, as a "reversal" of antic archetypes; and in *The Tempest* he contravenes the opposing "antic" magic of a "Dam," the witch Sycorax, who is Caliban's mother. The name Sycorax has been etymologized from the Greek korax (raven), an apparent epithet in the *Metamorphosis* for Medea, the Scythian raven.

In the antic masque of *The Masque of Queenes*, the Dam, an embodiment of discord, fears the return of a longed-for "*Age* of *Gold*" ruled over by Fame and Heroic "Vertue." And in the main masque after the Dam and her coven "quite vanishd" within the scenic Hell's mouth (l. 357), the harmonious Golden Age is restored with the appearance of the heroic female masquers and the winged figure Fame on top of her scenic House, a House decorated with statues of heroic figures including "Homer," "Virgil" and "Aeneas."

Though Jonson's masque obviously differs from *The Tempest* in structure and narrative, its wider themes and cosmic iconography involving magic, discord caused by fury, epic romance types and passages, Golden Age harmony and heroic virtue—all cast in a court theatrical work—apparently had a strong impact on Shakespeare's masque-like drama.

Along with being considered a romance, the genre of *The Tempest* has been viewed as a difficult-to-define blending of open masque spectacle with underlying, though largely concealed, Latin play form. To better clarify its genre, critics have searched for some novel theatrical work, a masque-like drama, to which it might be compared.

Both Enid Welsford and Frank Kermode focused on what at first might appear a surprising analogue: John Milton's *A Mask presented at Ludlow Castle,* popularly known as *Comus*. Their differing conclusions are of considerable interest because, in using *Comus* as a critical touchstone, they seem to be sensitively and almost instinctively responding to deep masque qualities in the two works, qualities relating, in my view, to magical "hinges," structured antic and harmonious episodes, culminating spectacle and final acted-out "presentations" that they do not probe or define. Rather, they make passing and extremely general comments on genre that are arresting because they set the critical stage for much of the confused commentary on *The Tempest* that has followed.

According to Kermode,

> *The Tempest* is a pastoral drama; it belongs to that literary kind which includes certain earlier English plays, but also and more significantly *Comus*.[24]

Welsford, avoiding the term "pastoral," considers both works "plays," but "plays . . . founded on an idea," the magical redress of wrong, rather than on the choreographic dances that she rightly sees as central to masques.[25] Overlooking the strong choreographic symbolism throughout *A Mask Presented at Ludlow Castle,* she argues that Milton's work is essentially a "dramatized debate." *The Tempest,* she claims, lacks such dramatized debate but is infused with a sense of wonder (318). Welsford thus startlingly concludes that the drama *The Tempest* is "more masque-like than *Comus*" (318).

In their comparisons, the two critics follow in the tradition of Samuel Johnson who, writing with lively if misguided rationalistic intensity after the demise of court masques, insisted that Milton's *A Mask Presented at Ludlow Castle* is a drama.[26] This view was widely and uncritically disseminated over the years, and in this century was echoed by Ronald Bayne in the many editions of the influential *Cambridge History of English Literature.* "*Comus* must not be classed as a masque because there is no disguising and no dancing," he remarks, ignoring the disguises of the Attendant Spirit, Comus, and central figures, and disregarding the concluding rural and court dances; "it is a species of outdoor entertainment and, therefore, akin to pastoral." He adds that *Comus,* as a kind of pastoral play, is an "offshoot of the legitimate drama" written for outdoor performance.[27] In the curious half-light of this sort of distorted designation of genre, attempts to clarify masque and classical elements in *The Tempest*—through comparison with *Comus,* and even with masques by Ben Jonson—have become all but hopelessly muddled.

Over the past 20 years, *Comus,* though containing a distinctive Miltonic argument between opposed typal figures, has increasingly been recognized as having the genre and form that Milton gave to it in title, in content, and in the "disposition" of its structural elements. It is an indoor "Mask," employing changeable scenery and stage machines, and featuring youthful aristocratic performers who, though briefly encountering heavenly and evil figures in pastoral disguise within a dark wood, finally symbolically unmask on being discovered and presented in Triumph to their noble parents, who are seated in state before a scenic representation of "Ludlow Town and the President's Castle."[28] It is a "Mask" too in having, not a five-act or Latin play structure, but rather a masque structure composed of a Prologue, an Antimasque, a Main Masque culminating in a modest spectacle (the "rising" of Sabrina and her nymphs on a chariot); a Presentation and symbolic unmasking of the youthful performers before the state chair of the Lord President of

Wales; a revels dance of Triumph by these aristocratic masquers, and then an Epilogue.[29]

Welsford says nothing about the antimasque-main masque form of Milton's *A Mask Presented at Ludlow Castle*. But in a general comment on the structure of *The Tempest* that has strongly influenced later critics, she states that Shakespeare introduces structural elements into his play—presumably antimasque and main masque episodes—possibly borrowed from Ben Jonson.

> [I]f Shakespeare is following Ben Jonson, he is following, not his theories as a classicist, but his practice as a writer of masques; he is, indeed, overcoming a difficult dramatic problem by making skillful use of typical masque construction. (338)

In Welsford's view, *The Tempest* is a play, but "not a classical play," embodying typical masque construction and characterized by a "spirit" of wonder "far nearer to the spirit of the masque than . . . *Comus*" (339–40). Most significant is her definition of that "spirit":

> It is the story behind the play, rather than the play itself which is dramatic; and the second scene of *The Tempest* has affinities with the masque induction rather than the Greek prologue. For classical drama, whether Greek or French, is concerned with the final phase of conflict, and the interest is concentrated upon the last few hours of uncertainty which must soon be terminated by irrevocable choice and decisive action; but the masque deals, not with the last phase of a conflict, but with a moment of transformation; it expresses, not uncertainty, ended by final success or failure, but expectancy, crowned by sudden revelation; and even when the opposition of good and evil is symbolized by masque and antimasque, this opposition is shown as a contrast rather than a conflict. It is in this respect that *The Tempest* is more masque-like than dramatic, for Prospero addresses Miranda in the tone of a masque presenter and, throughout the play, he manipulates the human characters as surely as he manipulates the spirit masquers. (339–40)

Asserting a dissenting position that he later modifies, Kermode approaches *The Tempest* as an academic pastoral drama:

> Miss Welsford's theory, that the play is more of a dramatized masque than a venture into classical dramatic structure, takes insufficient account of the fact that the play is divided into five acts in accordance with contemporary theory, and that its actions proceed in accordance with the scheme of classical development which the Renaissance commentators worked out in the tradition of Donatus and the later editors of Terence. (lxxiv)

In elucidating this supposed classical dramatic structure in an introduction to his edition of *The Tempest*, Kermode allows that there is "general influence from the court masque" on the play; but he insists that Shakespeare, at times deliberately concealing his true academic intentions, imposed a four-division Terentian form upon this work printed in five acts. It is Kermode's contention that in his last play Shakespeare seemingly abides by the classical "unities" of time, place and action and "reverts to something like the formal structure which he used in his earlier attempts at romantic comedy" (lxxiv).

Here, of course, Kermode refers to the well-known neo-Terentian divisions: the *prologue*, which consists of a prefatory event or discourse; the *protasis*, which explains the argument and introduces the main characters; the *epitasis*, which develops the main narrative actions and conflicts; and the *exode or catastrophe*, which brings the play to a comic or calamitous conclusion. By the early 1600s, these divisions were delineated so loosely and generally as to be applicable to plays of extraordinary diversity. Consider the explanation of them given by Shakespeare's fellow actor-playwright Thomas Heywood within a year of the first recorded performance of *The Tempest*. In his *Apology for Actors*, Heywood writes that comedies

> are distributed into foure parts, the *Prologue*, that is, the preface; the *Protasis*, that is, the proposition, which includes the first act, and presents the Actors; the *Epitasis*, which is

> the businesse and body of the Comedy; the last the *Catastrophe*, and conclusion. (F)

Kermode divides up and merges the five-acts of Shakespeare's work, as they appear in the 1623 Folio, to make the following four Latin play segments: *prologue* (act 1, scene 1); *protasis* (act 1.2 through act 2); *epitasis* (acts 3 through act 4); *catastrophe* (act 5).

Some straining is necessary, however, to make the drama fit even this very general Latin play pattern. The presentation of the key actors, which usually takes place compactly in the one-act *protasis* comprising the second division, is extended to other divisions in *The Tempest*. Kermode proposes a lengthy *protasis* and claims that the "presentment of the actors . . . is accomplished in the first act, save for Trinculo and Stephano, who appear in II, ii, as authority permitted" (lxxv). But key figures Alonso, Sebastian, Antonio and Gonzalo are introduced and directly set into action in the Prologue, the play's first division. Only Prospero, Miranda, Caliban, Ariel and Ferdinand appear in that part of act 1 that Kermode includes in the *protasis*.

Because the form and modes of this alleged *protasis* are also difficult to fit to those of a Latin play, Kermode next argues that an academic Shakespeare, shifting from one narrative mode to another in a possibly defective way, is seeking to hide the very structural source to which he is assumed to be reverting. Kermode suggests that the playwright, in allegedly imposing formal conventions, "conceals" the "studious origin" of the play's *protasis* in which Prospero removes his magic robes and speaks informally to his daughter Miranda. Shakespeare then stands critically accused of "an extraordinary though not perhaps successful attempt to provide a natural motivation and a naturalistic dialogue" (p. lxxv).

Kermode then claims that this same academic Shakespeare forces unmotivated action upon the play's *epitasis* for formalistic structural reasons. "The apparently unnecessary perturbation of Prospero at the thought of Caliban," writes

Kermode of events following the interrupted betrothal masque, "may be a point at which an oddly pedantic concern for classical structure causes it to force its way through the surface of the play" (lxxv). Similarly, according to Kermode, this academic Shakespeare, out of dedication to Latin play form, so strongly presses unmotivated action upon the *catastrophe* that a structural rent or tear seemingly appears in the play. After stating that Ariel "makes" Prospero say "he will offer his enemies forgiveness"—the Magus in conversation with Ariel, in fact, freely chooses virtue—Kermode adds that "Ariel's act is so unnecessary in view of the already existing comic motive—the betrothal of Ferdinand and Miranda—that it is hard to avoid seeing tears through the texture of the play." The critic then wavers, coming upon a possible but partial explanation of the motive that does not depend upon presumed Latin play form. "On the other hand," he writes, "the conversation about forgiveness, unlike Prospero's agitation at the prospect of Caliban's rebellion, has some motivation in the structure of the play's ideas" (lxxv).

If an oddly pedantic Shakespeare had, in fact, forced Latin play structure and conventions upon *The Tempest* in this stiffly academic fashion, it would indeed appear that the bard made an aesthetic mistake. The neo-Terentian form of *The Tempest*, as explained by Kermode, seems alternately disguised or "forced"; the motivation of characters in the play, unclear; the unanticipated shift to modes of masque-like antic action in scene ii, a deviation into a possibly defective naturalism. However, even Kermode finally appears to step back from his own Latin play thesis. After working his way through exceptions and distinctions, he ends by cautiously stating that it only "seems likely that Shakespeare deliberately constructed his play in accordance with neo-Terentian regulations" (lxxv–lxxvi). In my view, it is evident that only traces of formal Latin play structure used by Shakespeare in some of his early comedies appear in the *The Tempest*, and they appear uniquely merged, as will be seen, with masque-like theatrical forms.

In an essay written some years after the introduction, Kermode, finally taking into account comments by masque critic D. J. Gordon cited earlier in that introduction,[30] gives new weight to core masque structural and spectacle elements. Earlier remarks about *The Tempest* as a pastoral drama are dropped, and Kermode stresses the aristocratic nature of the key figures. Kermode now refers to Shakespeare's allegedly "close" rather than "seeming" "adherence to traditional five-act structures."[31] Yet in comments that in many ways echo those of Enid Welsford and D. J. Gordon, he writes that *The Tempest*

> has also a more general resemblance to the masque. Prospero is like a masque-presenter, and the castaways wander helpless in an enchanted scene under his spell, until he chooses to release them, drawing back a curtain to display a symbol of aristocratic concord, Ferdinand and Miranda at chess. At the climax of each subplot there is a spectacular contrivance that owes something to the masque. . . . Prospero's famous lament, "Our revels now are ended," echoes the regret conventionally expressed at the ephemeral nature of the incredibly costly furnishings of court masques. If we take all of this together with the close adherence to traditional five-act structures, we may conclude that Shakespeare was deliberately blending these 'tricks' with a conventional form that lent itself well to a necessarily intensive presentation of the material. (43)

In focusing ever more precisely on the drama's visionary shows, recent structural critics have advanced provocative if conflicting explanations of the function of the antic and harmonious spectacles, their unusual placement, and their possible meanings.

Concentrating on just the act 4 betrothal masque and Prospero's reaction to it, Robert Grudin interprets the Magus's vexed condition after the presentation, not as the forced intrusion of a Latin play climax by an "oddly pedantic" Shakespeare, but as an axial turn in the Magus's outlook giving form to the drama. The betrothal masque is seen to "mirror Prospero's desire, manifest throughout the first three acts, magically to redeem or civilize nature by banishing disruptive forces. . . ." The interruption of the masque is said to modify "this image by calling to mind, the figure of Caliban, a quality of nature that seems essentially irredeemable. . . ."[32] The Magus thus comes to a realization of "the ultimate limitation to human improvement of humanity," and there is a consequent "shift in emphasis from magic to providence" (408).

Although usefully highlighting this sudden turn in outlook and theme, Grudin's loosely argued interpretation leaves out climactic events in act 5, and offers no structural analysis of the play as a whole. But it points the way toward further exploration of the drama's masque-like form while avoiding the need to claim that an academic Shakespeare made, in the words of Grudin, "an almost childish error in dramatic fabric" (405).

Extending and expanding structural analysis to episodes and contexts not addressed by Grudin, Glynne Wickham and Richard Gilman have placed the spectacle visions, predominantly seen in act 4, against the background of Ben Jonson's invention of antimasque-main masque structure, an invention first explained, as has been noted, in Jonson's preface to the *Masque of Queenes* (1609). Jonson pointed out that at Queen Anne's command he first introduced an antic "foyle, or false-masque" showing an "ougly *Hell*" to counterbalance the later harmonious main masque showing the House of Fame. In the opening "false-masque," Jonson produced what he called a "spectacle of strangeness" in which witches, associated with the Furies, with dissonant sounds, grotesque movements, curious incantations and speeches, and wild dances performed before a scenic hell's mouth that flamed beneath and "smoakd vnto the top of the Roofe" (ll. 13–26). In the contrasting orderly main masque, the Queen and her ladies, representing the queens of ancient peoples, entered from the House of Fame, were presented to the state by the figure Fame, and performed graceful main masque dances.

Centering on the banquet vision in act 3, scene 3 and the

betrothal masque of act 4, Wickham argues that the two visionary shows read in sequence are examples of the new Jonsonian antimasque and main masque successfully integrated into the play. Wickham finds an antimasque—the "phantom banquet of act 3"—and a main masque—Ceres and Juno in "the heavenly vision of act 4"—both requiring stage machinery. He observes that "some ninety lines of dialogue divorce the antimasque from masque." The lines, Wickham claims, are "a necessary deviation to permit one set of characters to react to the first vision and then quit the stage in order to make way for those other characters who are to witness the second of Prospero's "high charms." Wickham nonetheless admits to the "remarkable fact that Shakespeare should have chosen to borrow this double-device within a year and a half of the invention of the antimasque," and Wickham adds that he suspects that Shakespeare, unlike Thomas Campion and Thomas Heywood, followed Ben Jonson and Inigo Jones in giving very specific allegorical meaning to characters, images and action."[33]

Ernest B. Gilman, without mentioning Wickham's analysis, claims in contrast that in *The Tempest* "Shakespeare engineers an exact reversal of the order of events in a Jacobean masque." Using Jonson's new antimasque and main masque structure as a model, Gilman focuses on the supposedly reversed position of two spectacles in act 4: the harmonious betrothal masque, and the later antic spectacle of the "dogs and hounds" chasing Caliban, Stephano and Trinculo. "Prospero's undermined masque," Gilman remarks of the disrupted masque, "becomes a delicately subversive maneuver . . . hinting at the bedazzled, insulated self-regard of such entertainments." But by leaving out any detailed consideration of the fifth-act harmonious spectacles, Gilman overstates his case in arguing that Shakespeare is "overtly undoing the form by presenting the triumph of Prospero's art explicitly as a masque, only to expose the end of the masque to the raw conspiracy that should have been disposed of at the start."

Gilman comments on Prospero's powerlessness and humanity in the Epilogue, but like Wickham offers no close reading of fifth-act events. Rather, he provides a theory, arising from the views of Freud and Wolfgang Iser, about the constant "new beginnings" based upon remembering, repeating, and acting through.[34]

The readings of Wickham and Gilman obviously consider the play in a somewhat piecemeal fashion. Each places special selective emphasis upon masque-like spectacles in acts 2 and 4—Wickham on the banquet vision and the betrothal masque, and Gilman on the betrothal masque and then the "hounds and dogs" masque that follows—and each therefore arrives at a different critical conclusion. The pervasive masque-like quality of the play is overlooked, and the reliance solely on Ben Jonson's masques for context is too limiting.

Wickham and Gilman properly call attention to Shakespeare's apparent awareness in 1610–11 of Jonsonian antimasque-main masque theory and practice. But as *Pericles, Cymbeline, The Winter's Tale* and *The Tempest* demonstrate, Shakespeare was imaginatively playing upon, altering, and finally transcending Jonsonian and other popular forms under the impact of contemporaneous theatrical theory and practice advanced by writers almost as well known as Jonson.

In considering the preceding readings as a whole, what should be clear is the resistance of *The Tempest* to the formal, structural and genre models being imposed upon it. Exceptions, qualifications and some inconsistencies inevitably intrude upon the patterns advocated; and critics are unable to agree on the play's overall form. With its vestiges of four-part Latin play form compromised by supposed tears in the structural fabric; with its actual five-part divisions in the 1623 Folio possibly a late superimposition by a hand other than Shakespeare's; with its ties to just some themes and some character-types in romance, pastoral, and tragecomic literary and theatrical works; and with its interwoven antic and harmonious masque-like visionary episodes interpreted in different substantive and structural ways, *The Tempest* emerges as a unique amalgam of Renaissance theatrical and literary forms in transition. Its structure, as T. W. Baldwin and R. A. Foakes have observed, is indeed original. But the nature of that originality requires further definition.

Two

Dramatic Designs and the Spectacle Triumph

On the final morning before the "cracking" of Prospero's spells on the sixth hour, the enchanter recalls how his magic called forth the rattling thunder and "mutenous winds" of furious storms (D. 16). The storms without have matched the enchanter's fury within, but now they have passed.

In the ninth scene of *The Tempest*, as courtly characters awaken from spells and move forward in choreographic-symbolic patterns, the Magus Prospero presides over a series of wondrous "discoveries," "presentations" and magical "releases" that afford insights into overlooked structures, imaginative themes and stage conditions influencing Shakespeare's play.

At this sixth hour of ever-brightening illumination "as morning steales upon the night," and as the cosmic harmonies of "solemne Ayre" are heard (D. 16), the spellbound nobles physically come to life in the choreographic manner of featured performers "discovered" in an iconographic stage tableau. They progress from frantic movements outside a magic circle, to charmed static postures within, and then to harmonious movements as the charm is broken. Their rational awakening is compared in Prospero's speeches to the rhythmic movements of nature. As the light of dawn rises in the East, so "their rising sences/Begin to chace the ignorant fumes that mantle/Their cleerer reason" (D. 16). And as "the approching tide/Will shortly fill the reasonable shore/That now lies foul and muddy," so too "Their understanding/Begins to swell" (D. 17).

Here at the climactic turn of action in the main plot Prospero renounces both his past fury and his magic; "with my nobler reason, gainst my furie/Doe I take part," he declaims to Ariel. "The rarer Action is/In virtue than in vengeance." He calls for "heauenly Musicke" to replace his "rough Magicke," a magic that gave external expression to this internal fury and included black magical rituals of resurrection (D. 16).

> . . . To the dread ratling Thunder
> Haue I giuen fire, and rifted Ioue's stowt Oke
> With his owne Bolt: The strong-bas'd promontorie
> Haue I made shake, and by the spurs pluckt vp
> The Pyne and Cedar.
>
> (D. 16)

Then, like a "presenter" in a court masque identifying noble performers at the moment of their unmasking, Prospero dramatically releases Antonio, Alonso, Sebastian, Gonzalo and various attendants from static enchantment within a drawn magical circle, and "presents" both himself and these characters in their true, underlying but previously concealed social roles. He then unexpectedly "discovers" and "presents" his daughter Miranda and Alonso's son Ferdinand playing at chess, and supervises the entry of all characters into the actual society depicted in the play. As in a masque in which the unmasked main performers are "released" from theatrical artifice into the immediate social environment of the masquing hall—leaving their movement into the wider social world beyond the hall until after night-long revels—so too the characters in the play are released into their immediate social surroundings, their movement into the wider society of Milan and Naples in Italy delayed until the coming day.

Masque components, together with the final "entries" and "releases," make Shakespeare's play more than simply a romance drama in which the innocent lovers Ferdinand and Miranda, following much comic confusion, are finally brought happily together. The entries and releases make *The Tempest* more too than simply a Renaissance "tragecomedy" ending in the reconciliation and the partial forgiveness and repentance of characters.

Though somewhat dramatic because of its traditional, "public theatre" confrontational action, internal conflict in a few characters, and formal reconciliation of contending figures in the final scene, *The Tempest* brilliantly fulfills an inner dynamic in certain plays of Shakespeare toward masque-like representation and form. In early comic works of confusion and reconciliation, such as *Love's Labour's Lost, Twelfth Night* and *A Midsummer Night's Dream*, Shakespeare—influenced by masques—dramatized the sudden, fifth-act unmaskings of characters and their final movement from realms of artifice, illusion, or dream into the "actual" society of the theatrical world. Shakespeare variously and subtly exploited the themes of comic unmasking and social entry throughout his career. But in *The Tempest*, following the composition of the great tragedies, the playwright altered theatrical modes. Now, potentially tragic fury, impelling conspiracy and murder, rather than comic confusion, is overcome by magic; characters are "unmasked" and a generally triumphant Magus, declaring that he will abandon his spells, moves at last with other central characters into a far from perfect social world. In *The Tempest* Shakespeare represents this movement with masque-like rituals, magic and thematic oppositions.

In this drama of multiple influences and meanings, it is the play's dominating qualities of wonder and surprise and revelation—the hinging of action on unexpected magical events; the unanticipated "discoveries" leading to the "entry" of aristocratic characters into the drama's social world—that unmistakably associates *The Tempest* with the genre of court masques and spectacles. In his early years as he began his development as a playwright, Shakespeare had "academically" employed traditional Terentian conventions and forms in plays such as *Two Gentlemen from Verona* and *The Comedy of Errors*. But after writing the early histories and the comedies and then the great tragedies of the middle period, Shakespeare, in his final 1608–11 "experimental" phase, under the influence of contemporaneous theatrical theory and practice, imaginatively transcends popular forms in works such as *Pericles, Cymbeline, The Winter's Tale* and *The Tempest*. Shakespeare's impulse to chide theatrical convention is also evident in lines in *King Lear*, a work performed before James I in 1608. In stinging mockery of the playwrights and players following pat forms, Edmund—admittedly an ironic and treacherous figure—comments on the "formula" entrance of his good brother Edgar in a way that suggests Shakespeare's own disruptive approach to rigid theatrical practices. "Pat: he comes like the Catastrophe of the old Comedie: my Cue is villanous Melancholly, with a sighe like Tom o' Bedlam" (D. 286).

In *The Tempest* Shakespeare moves beyond simply employing visionary spectacles as climaxes to subplots, dramatically adapting a masquing Triumph—the "revelation" of Prospero—as a climax of the play's main plot. As Prospero's revelations are prolonged to include "discoveries" of the "men of sin" and the central figures, the full Triumph substitutes for, yet functions together with, the traditional confrontational comic "catastrophe" of Terentian drama. Further, by interspersing harmonious and antic spectacles in balanced but unexpected ways throughout the play, Shakespeare shows his deep-rooted debts to "old pageant" structure derived from the continental *balet de cour* and the Elizabethan *intermezzo* masque.

Digressive *intermezzo* masques, like the *balet-de-cour*

spectacles, were usually loose constructions containing some kind of prologue or induction establishing a "hinge"; central speeches and songs developing from the "hinge" and intermingled with antic and harmonious interludes; and finally a harmonious main entry spectacle and Triumph expressed through all the theatrical arts and particularly through dance. In these works series of antic and harmonious masque episodes are intermingled, without the imposition of any fixed governing pattern to match the specific occasion and the central invention.

Beginning with the supposedly first English masque of 1512 as recorded in *Hall's Chronicle*, disguised noblemen regularly made surprise "entries," actually or symbolically unmasked, paced forward into the social realm of the hall, and there took out spectators in a dance revel.[1] The "entries" were later elaborated on with symbolic main masque ballets that generally idealized the royalist state by associating the harmonious movement of the aristocrats under a king with the harmonious movements of the universe under God. But the masques and entertainments sometimes took extraordinarily discursive forms. At the famed Entertainment for Elizabeth at Kenilworth during the summer of 1575, interspersed antic and harmonious spectacles, very loosely "hinged" on the visit of a Queen to King Arthur's supposed kingdom and ending without dances, were presented for 17 days in succession.[2] The Kenilworth entertainment followed the pattern of parallel French court spectacles that were extended over many days, spectacles such as that in Paris in 1572 which preceded the St. Bartholomew's Day Massacre and included the *Paradis d'Amour* scenic representation of a moving iconographic cosmos.[3]

In 1581 the French *Balet Comique de la Royne*, a work of thematically associated interludes linked by a relatively strong "hinge," gave international prominence to masquing theatrical form and influenced English writers. At the opening of the ballet, an escaped prisoner of Circe runs into the hall and speaks of the sorceress's evil spells. Alternating harmonious and antic spectacles follow as Circe comes from her palace three times to interrupt the proceedings, twice enchanting the main masquers. In the final Triumph, virtuous divinities descend and enter to overcome the spells, take Circe prisoner, and then present themselves and their prisoner to the King; then Naiads perform the final figured dances.[4]

By convention, French ballet spectacles contained numerous *intermezzi* and regularly featured magicians and enchanters, such as the sorceress Medea. The ballets included *Au Ballet de Madame de Rohan*, in which the second part (1593) "hinged" on Medea casting spells over virtuous Nymphs and heroic Chevaliers; the *Ballet de Cupidon* (1605) in which Love is crucified and central figures are compared to Medea and Penelope; the *Ballet des Argonautes* (1614) centered on Circe's magical control of Jason and his crew; the *Ballet Danse a Rome par des Cavalliers Francois* (1615), performed in Venice, and containing a "Balet des Chavalliers Enchantez"; and the *Grand Ballet du Roy sur L'Adventure de Tancrede en la Forest Enchantèe* (1619), cast with 137 dancers, in which the French King, in the role of Tancred, breaks the enchantments of the magician Ismen. The *Ballet des dix Verds* (1615), celebrated the triumph of spring over winter and contained character-types representing the natural world; and the four elements danced in the *Ballet d'Armida* (1617).[5]

In England both Queen Anne and her successor Queen Henrietta Maria, aware of the fashionable and widely reported *balet-de-cour* spectacles, particularly at the French court,[6] took action to insure that *intermezzo* shows and spectacles of strangeness would be incorporated into Whitehall productions. As Ben Jonson recorded, Anne believed that the "life of these Spectacles lay in theyr variety"; and she "commaunded" Jonson, it will be recalled, to put "some Daunce, or shew" into the *Masque of Queenes* as a "foyle" for later episodes. "I was carefull to decline not," Jonson adds, implying that he had no choice.[7] Henrietta Maria also demanded that a "variety of Scenes, strange aparitions,

Songs, Musick and dancing of severall kinds" be included in William Davenant's masque *Luminalia*.[8] With variety in spectacle given this kind of preference at Whitehall, it is entirely possible that Shakespeare composed an original masque-like play with integral visionary spectacles, not only as a consequence of his normal development as a playwright, but also as a consequence of court pressures or even royal commands. In previous years by order of Queen Elizabeth, Shakespeare, after all, had restored Falstaff to life following his theatrical death in *Henry V* for a featured role in *The Merry Wives of Windsor*.

Like Shakespeare, Jonson sought to carry out royal theatrical commands. Yet Jonson's efforts to contrive a new masque form by balancing an opening antic spectacle of disorder against a concluding harmonious main masque, though widely influential at the time, was finally undermined by Court Architect Inigo Jones, who favored "old pageant" *intermezzo*-type masques stressing interludes and scenic spectacle. In the 1630s Jonson was dismissed as a court masque writer after a dispute with Jones over whether poetry or scenic spectacle was the controlling art, the so-called "soul" of the masque. In *An Expostulation with Inigo Jones*, Jonson bitterly mocked Jones's belief that scenic iconography conveyed deeper meanings than verse, that the eye of the beholder was surprised with delight and most profoundly enlightened through a staged, moving "speaking picture." "O shows! Shows! Mighty shows!" Jonson ironically exclaimed, "The Eloquence of masques! What need of prose,/Or verse, or sense, to express immortal you?" Raging against an iconographic art that he himself had championed in notes to early masques, Jonson acidly adds:

Tis true
Court hieroglyphics, and all arts afford
In the mere perspective of an inch-board,
You ask no more than certain politic eyes,
Eyes that can pierce into the mysteries
Of many colours, read them, and reveal
Mythology there painted on a slit deal.
Oh, to make boards to speak! There is a task![9]

After the dismissal of Jonson, writers submissive to the court architect again produced long *intermezzo*-type shows without a strong central hinge and without strong integral structure. In later works such as James Shirley's *The Triumph of Peace* (1634), Thomas Carew's *Coelum Britannicum* (1634) and William Davenant's *Britannia Triumphans* (1638), an increasing number of antimasques were introduced and ostentatious stagecraft featured. Elements of episodic "old pageant" shows thus made a comeback at court. Yet years earlier in *The Tempest*, Shakespeare had anticipated or had otherwise been directed into a movement toward such shows—really continuing in the main stream of "old pageant" continental tradition—by incorporating diverse *intermezzi* into a play also having iconographic spectacle.

When concern over printed act divisions and supposed "academic" form in *The Tempest* diminishes, the play's "spectacles of strangeness"can be seen as integral to the drama's overall theme and structure. Serving as climaxes to crucial turns in the main and subplots, the masque-like iconographic spectacles emphasize transcendent values of good and evil and afford insight into the internal ideals, impulses, conflicts and moral inclinations of the characters. They are placed late in the drama as emotional and thematic "peaks"—amazing staged magical disclosures—and would have been recognized as such by persons who possessed an immediate awareness of the "wonder" and iconographic figuration of court presentations. To experienced Whitehall spectators, the startling visions—rendered through the combined theatrical arts of costume design, music, choreographic movements, sound effects and speeches—would have gone much further to define the play than would an awareness of Latin play structure.

The play's first "spectacle of strangeness" occurs after the opening Prologue scene, which shows the furious storm unleashed by Prospero's magic, as the Magus himself enters in an Induction (D. 2) that functions as part of a masque-like structural "frame" for the play. In the Induction, Prospero briefly removes his magic mantle, revealing himself in his humanity as a somewhat inadequate father. This foreshadowing and partial "unmasking" in scene 2 is structurally balanced against the full climactic "unmasking" and relative Triumph of Prospero, as the true Duke of Milan and as an aging human being, in the last scene of the drama.

The noisy Prologue storm scene spectacle that opens the play, and the moving Epilogue speech by Prospero that ends it, also "frame" the drama and the Magus's "unmasking." The last lines of the play, disclosing a vulnerable Prospero, cast the beginning tempest scene and the entire play's iconography and action into stark perspective. Dramatized is the full "metamorphosis" of Prospero from a Magus of fury and controlled power—the magical creator of a fearful tempest that is constrained in that it does no harm—to an old but virtuous man in need of prayers, his fury and magical force supplanted by a submission to divine providence.

The sea-tempest scene, in depicting desperate ship passengers and rebellious drunken mariners, functions too as a broad icon of the fear and fury that drive characters to chaotic action. As an antic spectacle—complete with conventional Whitehall stage effects rendering the crash of thunder probably accompanied by the flash of lightning—it thematically resembles the antic, opening scene of Jonson's *Masque of Queenes* in which, "Haggs or Witches" representing furies dance wildly before a scenic Hell's mouth "flaming beneath" and smoking "unto the top of the Roofe" (7.282, ll. 25–26).

Between the partial and full unmasking of Prospero, the body of *The Tempest* contains typical spectacle action as rebellious noble characters, under the influence of the Magus's spells and Ariel's manipulative direction, wander as in a maze and fall at last into an enchanted sleep. The attire of the wandering performers, like the originally designed and new-dyed garments of main masquers, has about it a shimmering resilience. "Our garments, being, (as they were) drencht in the sea," Gonzalo states, "hold notwithstanding their freshness and glosses, being rather new dy'de then stain'd with salt water" (D. 6).

In a generally parallel subplot, Caliban is pivotal among antic character-types—Stephano, Trinculo, the Boatswain, the seamen and even, at times, Ariel—in functioning as the most antithetical masque-like figure of discord opposing Prospero's control of characters and events. Caliban as a character springs from antimasque grotesque types. In the manner of Bacchus and other tipsy figures of excess in masques, he becomes drunk along with seamen Stephano and Trinculo while wandering with them over the island. The conspiracy to kill Prospero, though seriously intended and pursued by Caliban and his cohorts, loses intensity because the subplot is intermingled with these episodes of drunken, antic physical humor of the sort evident in masques. In seeking to murder Prospero and obtain possession of the isle with the help of the seamen, the monster causes the enchanter's mental and imaginative "distraction"; but, as in a masque, Caliban remains throughout under the magical power of this main character-type. At the conclusion of scene 8, Caliban is driven off the stage in defeat, leaving the extended final scene primarily for Prospero's Triumph over and reconciliation with his former aristocratic enemies. Only in the play's last 70 lines are the subplot figures brought on stage and quickly included in a more general reconciliation.

Increasingly in recent years, Caliban has been found a sympathetic and, in some instances, an admirable and heroic character, particularly by contemporary commentators stressing wide-ranging intertextual political issues of colonialism, slavery and oppression. These critics stress that this temporarily enslaved subject is forced to carry logs under the insults of a harsh master, a supposed type of a tyrannical European colonizer. "Malignant Thing" (D. 4), Prospero cries at the creature, "Filth" (D. 5), "poysonous slaue" (D. 4), "Hag-seed" (D. 5) "bastard" (D. 18), "demy-diuell" (D. 19).

Critics quote poignant statements by Caliban to reveal the creature's underlyling "human" emotions and frustrations. In a constantly cited passage, Caliban seeks to shield the seamen Stepheno and Trinculo from fear and displays a surprising pleasure in what is termed "sweet" music:

> Be not affeard. The Isle is full of noyses,
> Sounds, and sweet aires that giue delight and hurt not.
> (D. 12)

There is genuine pathos in Caliban's dull perception of the gross and drunken Stephanos and Trinculo as admirable figures, possibly even otherworldly beings. "These be fine things," the monster says, ". . . if they be not sprights" (D. 10). The creature's feelings, it has been noted, appear to reflect those attributed in popular travel lore to New World natives. These were people said to have been astounded by their first sight of seemingly divine Europeans, and men reportedly quick to become drunk on the strangers' liquor. What needs to be added, however, is that in masque and spectacle tradition beginning with the French *Balet Comique* (1585), it became conventional for antic or other figures entirely to misjudge the spiritual natures of strange evil or virtuous character-types who unexpectedly appear from varied heavenly, demonic, or earthly realms of the iconographic theatrical universe, character-types who are falsely "elevated" in stature and often undeservedly worshipped as gods or goddesses. These strange, evil character-types traditionally use herbs or liquors to lure victims into beastly actions. In Milton's *A Mask Presented at Ludlow Castle*, for example, a fallacious spiritual elevation occurs when the antic enchanter Comus considers the virtuous human Lady with her "Divine enchanting ravishment" a "Goddess," and her two human Brothers "a faery vision,/ Of some gay creatures of the element/That in the colors of the Rainbow live."[10] In an attempt spiritually to corrupt the Lady and to make her his Queen, Comus tries unsuccessfully to tempt her into drinking a magic liquor that would her transform into a beast-headed monster.

In *The Tempest* this type of masque-like iconography and action is adeptly interposed within the drama and infused with memorable emotional significance. An innocent

Miranda delights in her first vision of Ferdinand and mistakenly "elevates" the virtuous human youth with his "braue forme" to "a thing diuine" (D. 5). In the final scene of the play, she again delights in and mistakenly "elevates" the generally repentant former enemies of Prospero into beings from a brave new world. The hapless Caliban in the parallel but antithetical subplot succumbs to the temptation of Stephano's supposed "Celestiall liquor" and emotionally adores the intoxicated seaman as a "braue god." "I will kneele to him," says Caliban after tasting the liquor (D. 10). The monster goes further, swearing religious and political fealty to this tottering sailor who wishes to make himself the island's "King" with Miranda as his "Queene" (D. 12). "Ile kisse thy foot," Caliban declares, "Ile sweare my selfe thy Subiect" (D. 10). Caliban's gestures of adoration and obedience are on their face so sadly absurd that they even elicit a plaintive comment from Trinculo. "A most rediculous Monster," the seaman remarks, "to make a wonder of a poore drunkard." (D. 10).

Considering such commonly excerpted lines in the light of masque antic iconography and the play's contexts provides fuller insight into Caliban's basic character and role. Although colonial, New World, and even medieval "strange-race" resonances arise from Caliban's representation, he is not directly depicted in the subplot as a human native of the New World or of any recognizable colonized land. In the tradition of frequently ignored court iconography, Caliban appears as a subhuman being on a masque-like magical Mediterranean island inhabited by spirits and a castaway magician and his daughter, a being having considerable dimension who is nonetheless closely associated with the antic masque character-type base "Earth" (D. 4).

In 1609 in Jonson's *The Masque of Queene's* the traditional antic character-type Earth, depicted as "at warres" with the other more spiritual elements, seeks to give birth to cosmic disorder under the magical power of Witches in league with the "Deuil" (7.295–96, ll. 228–53). "Dame Earth shall quake," the Witches chant, pouring magical liquors on the ground to promote the strange nativity, "And the Houses shake,/And her Belly shall ake,/As her Back were brake" (7.296 ll. 255–58). The antic ceremonies are disrupted and the birth prevented only by the sudden entrance of virtuous main masquers.

In the subplot of *The Tempest*, Caliban, as a basic type, is a masque-like antic figure of earthly disorder born of a witch and, in the words of Prospero, sired by the Devil; but the creature as an individualized figure demonstrates a capacity for positive spiritual growth. According to Prospero, the pregnant witch Sycorax, banished from Algiers for unnamed crimes, was "hither brought with child" and "left by th' Saylors" (D. 4). Sycorax, in giving birth to a "bastard" creature (D. 18), Prospero explains, "did littour heere/, A freklld whelpe hag-borne) not honour'd with/a humane shape" (D. 4). Sycorax's commands were so "earthy, and abhord," Prospero adds, that the delicate spirit Ariel could not obey them (D. 4).

In statements that Caliban confirms, Prospero explains how he nurtured the creature with "humane care" and "lodg'd" Caliban in his "owne Cell" (D. 5). "I lou'd thee," Caliban confesses to the magician, speaking of that early period when Prospero taught him "how/To name the bigger Light, and how the lesse/That burne by day, and night" (D. 4). But Prospero angrily assails Caliban for a betrayal of trust. Charged by the magician with having attempted physically to "violate" Miranda, the unrepentant creature continues to displays a churlish delight in the attack.

> Oh ho, Oh ho, would't had bene done:
> Thou didst preuent me: I had peopel'd else
> This Isle with *Calibans.*
>
> (D. 5)

This gross delight is registered despite Miranda's past kindness in nurturing and educating Caliban. As Miranda says to the creature,

> I pittied thee,
> Took pains to make thee speak, taught thee each houre

> One thing or other: when thou didst not (Sauage)
> Know thine owne meaning; but wouldst gabble, like
> A thing most brutish, I endow'd thy purposes
> With words that made them knowne:
>
> (D. 5)

The magician and his daughter had not in any traditional sense attempted to "colonize" Caliban by supplanting and so destroying his native culture and language. Before the pair arrived, in Miranda's account, the monster had no language and no understanding of his own meanings or aims. Caliban, moreover, had shown no capacity to rule either himself or others. Neither had Prospero or Miranda, as castaways, made material claims to the island as a physical "possession," althrough the enchanter has exercised human rule by magic over subhuman Caliban and the spirit inhabitants. It is Caliban who, though born of a witch recently banished to the isle, argues for physical possession against possible claims by others, including presumed long-term spirit residents: "This Iland's mine by *Sycorax* my mother" (D. 4).

Prospero and Miranda have sought unsuccessfully to lift Caliban's "most brutish" nature closer to a human level through nurturing and the teaching of a "first" language, but their efforts have largely failed. The creature has turned with hostility against their instruction just as he has turned physically against Miranda. In scene 2, Caliban, mocking the benefits of learning, avers with a flash of anger, "my profit on't/Is, I know how to curse" (D. 5). The further regression of Caliban takes place in scene 4 in the presence, not of Prospero, but of the corrupt and manipulative Stephano. Under Stephano's antic drunken tutelage, Caliban adopts a debased and beastly language learned from "Celestial liquor." "Here is that which will giue language to you, Cat," says Stephano, holding up a bottle (D. 9). The tempted creature drinks and soon utters words of violence and murder. "Beate him enough,"the monster declaims as Stephano strikes Trinculo, "after a little time Ille beate him too" (D. 12). Of his teacher Prospero, Caliban remarks, "Batter his skull, or paunch him with a stake/Or cut his wezand with thy knife" (D. 12).

Given the underlying typal association of this subhuman creature with base matter, his pleasure in recalling an attempted rape, and his vicious impulses toward brutality and acted-out plans for murder, Prospero is justified in restraining Caliban.[11] For in the body of the subplot, the unfolding characterization of Caliban as an antic conspiratorial figure is rendered with pathos, but is not essentially sympathetic. Only after Caliban is magically punished by Prospero in scene 8—furious beasts pursue the monster off stage—does he register a character change. Upon reentering at the end of scene 9, Caliban shows an imprint of "goodnesse" in being jolted, after beholding the seemingly wondrous transformation of the Magus into the Duke of Milan, into a desire for reconciliation with Prospero. This unexpected resolution, contrived in its suddenness, is made at least plausible by Caliban's admission in scene 2 of past "love" for the enchanter and by the creature's past demonstrated if misdirected religious impulses. In the final moments of the drama, Caliban is seized by a desire for wisdom and grace.

At climactic points in the main and subplots, integral spectacles of "strangenesse" serve as dramatic fulcrums. In two antic visions in scene 7, the usurpers Antonio and Sebastian, whom Ariel had earlier thwarted in their plot to murder Alonso and Gonzalo, are startled, exposed and contained. The two magical interludes decisively "lever" the play away from possible tragic denouements of revenge and murder. During the first vision, Prospero is said to be "on the top (invisible:)," that is, in court theatrical terminology, at the highest, most commanding position in the Whitehall scenic heavens wearing iconographic "weeds" designed to signify invisibility. Apparitional shapes on the stage below—shapes that the iconography implies are subject to the Magus's power, given his "top" hierarchical position—carry a banquet into view and then, with inviting motions while dancing, beckon the conspirators forward toward false delights which remain out of reach (D. 13). Through the staged action of this iconographic speaking picture, presented to the sounding of "*Solemne and strange Musicke,*" the conspirators' inner impulses to temptation are both disclosed and frustrated (D. 13).

In the second vision later in the scene, the tempting banquet is again on stage before the conspirators, luring them onward, but in this episode they are mocked, stunned and completely overcome. "*Thunder and Lightning*" open the magical vision, and again would have been rendered on the Whitehall stage with special effects. Ariel is then said to "Enter" in the guise of a Harpy. According to the stage directions, Ariel "*claps his wings upon the Table*" and the tempting banquet, like the shattered hope of the plotters, "*vanishes*" before it can be tasted (D. 13).

As a self-declared "minister of Fate," Ariel powerfully denounces the "men of sin" and "*vanishes in Thunder,*" possibly through an available stage trap as stage "thunder" rumbles. The apparitional shapes enter, this time to dance with derisive "*mockes and mowes*" before leaving the stage, carrying off the banquet table. The stage directions are silent in this episode on whether Prospero remains "on the top" in his weeds of invisibility; as a Magus whose fury is manifest in the creation of the interlude and its figures, he possibly stayed in the summit position.

Counterpoised against these antic visions that destroy, through their sheer magical power, the conspirators' dreams of sinful possession and dominance, there appear at the end of scene 8 and in scene 9 those essentially harmonious spectacle Triumphs. These magically confirm and disclose the virtuous ideals, motivations and dreams of Prospero, Miranda and Ferdinand, with limitations imposed by the actual social world depicted in the play. Near the end of scene 8, the betrothal masque of peace and fecundity points the way thematically toward a final resolution of action in virtue rather than fury. But the masque is interrupted before a complete Triumph is realized. The culmination of virtuous action thus takes place in the last scene with the unmasking of "Prospero" and his former enemies, who join together in reconciliation; and with the "discovery" of Ferdinand and Miranda playing chess.

Following the "betrothal masque" in scene 8 but before the "unmasking" of Prospero in scene 9, one more antic spectacle is introduced in *intermezzo* fashion, yet in ways that make it integral to the drama. This is the noisy and chaotic driving off stage of Caliban, Trinculo and Stephano, who are pursued by "*Spirits in Shape of Dogs and Hounds*" whose viciousness match the viciousness of the characters (D. 16). This magical iconographic punishment, meted out against seditious figures who are drenched from wading in a "filthy" pool, completely ends their dreams of killing Prospero and gaining riches. They are, as Prospero declares at the end of scene eight, at his "mercy" as are all his enemies (D. 16). What remain for the final scene, then, are Prospero's climactic magical Triumphs of disclosure, but Triumphs that in *The Tempest* are restricted by human mortality and imperfection.

When considered in the light of masques and court spectacles and of *intermezzo*-type theatrical works, the scenes and visionary episodes in *The Tempest*, a play showing traces of Latin play form, fall into a unique structural pattern: a Prologue and induction; antic episodes of conspiracy and confused "mazy" wanderings; Spectacles of Strangeness magically ending the conspiracy and serving as fulcrums of action; Triumphs involving the "unmasking," reconciliation and reentry into society of the central figures; and a final Epilogue.

What becomes evident is an original masque-like dramatic form, one balancing opening, and potentially tragic, episodes of antic disorder against final Triumphs of social reintegration. Central spectacles of a varied *intermezzo* kind, moreover, turn the work from motifs of vengeance to those of virtue. Yet by including a closing speech by Prospero about a return to Milan in scene 9, following the Triumphs, and then a somber Epilogue, Shakespeare, abandoning the harmonious final court ballet and the revels found in masques, cuts through idealizing elements in the spectacle tradition to carry action back to an imperfect world.

The overall form of the play, "hinged" on Spectacles of Strangeness intermeshed with vestiges of Latin play structure, falls into the following structural patterns:

DRAMATIC SPECTACLE TRIUMPH STRUCTURE	*Scenes followed by Folio Act and Scene Divisions*	*VESTIGES OF CONVENTIONAL STRUCTURE*
PROLOGUE		PROLOGUE
Introductory scene: Disorder and Tempest *"Enter a Ship-master, and a Boteswaine"*	*scene 1 (1.1)*	
The magician-presenter's Induction: Prospero partially "unmasks" as a human being before his daughter Miranda "Enter Prospero and Miranda"	*scene 2 (1.2)*	PROTASIS
ANTIC DRAMATIC ACTION: A POTENTIAL TRAGEDY IS AVERTED BY PROSPERO'S MAGIC		
Antic disorder: "lost" wandering movements on the island maze; Ferdinand is believed drowned; plans for sedition and murder; restraining enchantments		
Ariel prevents the attempted murder of Alonso and Gonzalo, who have fallen into an enchanted sleep	*scene 3 (2.1)*	
Caliban carries logs and, becoming drunk, joins with the antic seamen Stephano and Trinculo	*scene 4 (2.2)*	

Ferdinand is enchanted and, out of love for Miranda, performs Caliban's work in carrying logs	*scene 5 (3.1)*	EPITASIS
Caliban, Trinculo, and Stephano plan Prospero's murder, then follow strange "sounds"	*scene 6 (3.2)*	

DRAMATIC TURNING POINTS IN SPECTACLES OF STRANGENESS: POTENTIALLY TRAGIC ACTION ENDS AND AN INTERRUPTED BETROTHAL MASQUE POINTS THE ACTION TOWARD CONCLUDING SPECTACLE TRIUMPHS

Spectacle One: A conspiracy of aristocrats is frustrated when a magical banquet vanishes	*scene 7 (3.3)*
Spectacle Two: The conspiracy is ended by a vision of Ariel as a Harpy denouncing the aristocratic "men of sin"	*scene 7 (3.3)*
Spectacle Three: A visionary betrothal masque is interrupted when Prospero remembers Caliban's conspiracy	*scene 8 (4.1)*
Spectacle Four: The conspiracy of Caliban, Trinculo, and Stephano is ended by the spectacle of "Spirits in the shape of dogs and hounds" pursuing the plotters off stage	*scene 8 (4.1)*

SPECTACLE TRIUMPHS OF VIRTUE: THE ENTRIES, UNMASKING, AND RECONCILIATION IN WONDER OF THE CENTRAL FIGURES		COMIC CATASTROPHE
Prospero to "Solemn music" with his magical powers at their "zenith," releases nobles from enchantments in a charmed circle; theatrically "unmasks" before the nobles by changing magic robes for court clothing; and is reconciled to the nobles, whose true identities as past usurpers are revealed	*scene 9 (5.1)*	
Prospero "discovers" Miranda and Ferdinand playing chess in a brief spectacle of revelation. Prospero and all others join hands. Ariel magically leads seamen awakened from enchantments to Prospero, and also drives Caliban, Trinculo and Stephano before the Magus. All of the principal figures are reconciled, with Prospero telling the nobles they should prepare for departure to Naples "in the morn"	*scene 9 (5.1)*	
EPILOGUE		EPILOGUE
Prospero, now without his magical powers, further "unmasks" to the audience as a human being and also as an actor. He asks to be "released" by the applause of the audience to go to Naples, and he asks too for "prayers" so that his ending will not be "despair."		

Viewed from this different structural perspective, which calls special attention to the interrelationship of the play's unfolding episodes rather than to act divisions that were possibly added after Shakespeare's death, the magical banquet spectacles in scene 7 are not so dramatically removed from the betrothal masque in scene 8. Similarily, the broken-off masque in scene 8 accordingly is better resolved in the scene 9 revelation of Prospero, and the "discovery" of the characters Miranda and Ferdinand playing the battle-game of chess. Previously cited "colonial" elements that some critics have recently claimed to be the "center" of the play—for example, Prospero's harsh and allegedly tyrannical treatment of his "slave" Caliban; the plying of Caliban by foreign seamen with intoxicating liquor; and the "revolt" of Caliban against Miranda and Prospero—are contained within the wider context of the Mediterranean magical-island setting. These largely "antic" subplot elements can be seen to serve as a counterpoint to final "harmonious" main plot action, culminating in betrothal and reconciliation.

The play's spectacle structure, allowing for a fluid acting out of events in the time required for performance, without any need for act breaks, exactly accords with the fluid manner of masque presentation. The spectacle structure, in fostering such continuous action, is also in accord with all the other masque-like components of the play: the iconographic setting; the "descent" of a goddess from the heavens; the seemingly choreographic movements of performers in a maze; the strange masque-like songs; the emphasis in speeches upon the transience of life; the ritualistic action featuring visions and a magical release; and the final triumphant "unmasking" of underlying identities.

Thus, Shakespeare's transitional drama can be seen, in the context of so-called romance theatrical works of the late sixteenth century and the early seventeenth, as a special development of romance Trage-Comedies and varied masque and spectacle forms. In this dramatized Spectacle Triumph, traditional stage-play conflicts, centered on anguish or uncertainty ending in tragic catastrophe or reconciliation, are partly subsumed in spectacle forms and largely resolved through the wonders of magic. Motivation is illumined and conflict represented, not only through the dramatic device of anguished soliloquies or confrontational dialogue and action, but through the device of mysterious symbolic spectacles projecting "present fancies." The destructive fury of a noble or heroic figure, fury that would normally lead to a tragic "fall," is overcome by the impulse to virtue, an impulse given substance by the figure's magical control of events in a realm apart from the normal social world. In the dramatized Spectacle Triumph, the action culminates with the magical victory of the central figure in the controlled realm, then with the revelatory "unmasking" of the social nature of the figure, and finally with the entry of that figure from "undreamed shores" into an actual society—whatever its condition—as represented in the play. What is important is that the central noble or heroic figure, beyond being reconciled to others, does triumph over internal destructive impulses and external destructive forces using magic.

Like Renaissance court masques that, in depicting the triumph of Princes rather than their fall, were considered the opposite of tragedy, the conclusion of *The Tempest* uniquely celebrates princely victory over tragedy, and the human revelation in the mortal world, of the sometimes harsh but ultimately virtuous Prospero.

1. *Painting of Lady Lucy Harington, Countess of Bedford, standing before a scenic cloud in the role of a Power of Juno in Ben Jonson's masque* Hymenaei *(1606). Lady Harington, who appeared with the figure Juno as one of the goddess's internal "faculties," was one of eight levitated main masquers who "descended" from the theatrical heavens down to the stage of the Whitehall Masquing House. In the betrothal masque in scene eight of* The Tempest, *the figure Juno appears in the heavens and, according to the Folio stage directions and the text, slowly "descends" during 30 lines of dialogue spoken by masque figures.*

Oil on canvas, attributed to John de Critz.
By permission of R. J. Berkeley, Berkeley Castle.
Courtesy of the Courtauld Institute of Art.

2. *The costume of Iris, goddess of the rainbow, is worn by Queen Elizabeth I in this famed "Rainbow" Portrait (c. 1600) attributed to Marcus Gheeraerts. The character Iris, who regularly appeared in masques at court, acts as a figure of divine harmony in the betrothal masque in act 4 of* The Tempest.

By permission of the Marquess of Salisbury, Hatfield House.

3. *Designs for Juno (left) and Iris (right) by Inigo Jones for Ben Jonson's masque* Chloridia *(1631). These two typal figures, introduced by Shakespeare into the betrothal masque in* The Tempest, *were also featured in masques at court, with Juno appearing with Iris in Ben Jonson's* Hymenaei *(1606), and earlier with Ceres and other goddesses in Samuel Daniel's* The Vision of the 12. Goddesses *(1604).*

Devonshire Collection, Chatsworth.
By permission of the Chatsworth Settlement Trustees.
Courtesy of the Courtauld Institute of Art.

The Tragicall Hiſtory of the Life and Death of *Doctor Fauſtus.*

Written by *Ch. Marklin.*

LONDON,
Printed for *Iohn Wright*, and are to be ſold at his ſhop without Newgate, at the

4. *The frontispiece for Christopher Marlowe's* The Tragicall History of D. Faustus *(1616) showing typical magical garments and implements of a kind used by Prospero in* The Tempest*: the robe, wand, book, and mystic circle.*

5. *Self-portrait by Inigo Jones, the stage designer and "Chief Surveyor and Architect of His Majesties Works" who is named in chapter 4 as one among the persons possibly signified by the character Prospero.*

The impact of Jones's stage illustions at Whitehall—with their moving scenic representations of an iconographic cosmos, their magical appearances and "fading" disappearances of characters, and their multiple levitations of performers and objects seemingly in space—is reflected in allusions to "wonders" in The Tempest *and is registered in the early masque commentary of Ben Jonson.*

Devonshire Collection, Chatsworth.
By permission of the Chatsworth Settlement Trustees.
Courtesy of the Courtauld Institute of Art.

6. *A typal antic Earthly Spirit costume, with a skin coat of scale-like protuberances and a hat showing vernal or wooded growth, by Inigo Jones for William Davenant's masque* The Temple of Love *(1635).*

In The Tempest *Caliban, who is called "thou Earth," is said by Stephano to be "legg'd like a man, and his fins like arms." Stephano then states that "this is no fish, but an islander." The lines raise the possibility that Caliban wore for one or both of the play's known Whitehall productions a typal "Earth" skin coat of seemingly sea-green scales, made with what appeared to be "fins" for arms, and with earthly or other icons highlighting the "fins." The monster "legg'd like a man" would not, however, have had on scale-like trousers of a kind shown in Jones's design.*

Devonshire Collection, Chatsworth.

7. *Airy Spirit (left) and Watery Spirit (right) costumes by Inigo Jones for* The Temple of Love *(1635). The Airy and Watery Spirits were traditional spectacle types who also appeared in* Somerset's Masque *(1613), presented in the English court together with* The Tempest *to celebrate the marriage of Princess Elizabeth, and in productions of the French* balet de cour. *In* The Tempest *the spirit Ariel, who along with earthly Caliban serves the magician Prospero, changes in scene two from his airy costume into the garb of a water nymph, and then again dons his airy habit later in the play.*

Devonshire Collection, Chatsworth.

8. *Typal French ballet figures of water (upper left) and fire (front center), the last played by the king, in the first entry of the* Ballet d' Armide.
By permission of the Bibliotheque Nationale Ob 1617 (Ob[1]).

Three

Performance Allusions and Whitehall Staging

In a pivotal article that has dominated recent critical-scholarly assumptions about the earliest productions of *The Tempest*, Gerald Eades Bentley, writing for the inaugural 1948 issue of the *Shakespeare Survey*, argued that around 1608 the King's Men decided their acquisition of the Blackfriars Theatre required the "devotion of Shakespeare's full-time energies to the Blackfriars instead of the Globe." This decision, Bentley maintained—taking exception to what he called 150 years of contrary opinions on the subject—caused Shakespeare to write "a new kind of play for the new theatre and audience . . . first he wrote *Cymbeline* for them, then, with greater dexterity in his new medium, *The Winter's Tale*, and finally, triumphant in his old mastery, *The Tempest*."[1]

Bentley's arguments rested on a wealth of historical information of a practical kind. Shakespeare, as a shareholder, was said to have written his final play for Blackfriars, generally stressing the music and poetry suitable to the indoor theatre, because the King's Men would earn more from admissions there—an argument Bentley found to be "most compelling." The company shareholders, he suggested, realized that "the real future of the theatrical profession in London lay with the court and the court party in private theatres" and that Shakespeare as a playwright could "most effectively" address this audience in the newly acquired theatre at Blackfriars (47).

Bentley noted the kinds of plays that had been staged at Blackfriars and the dates of their production, and he discussed in a general way how these dramas had tended to accentuate verse and song, as does *The Tempest*. But he centered his practical conjectures on what the King's Men Company shareholders would have decided was most to their economic and theatrical advantage. He did not closely analyze the text of *The Tempest* against specific staging conventions at Blackfriars or the Globe. Court staging practices were not considered at all. Yet the view that *The Tempest* was composed for Blackfriars presentation, with the Globe often added as well, has entered into mainstream Shakespeare commentary, and has had a strong influence upon criticism and scholarship on the early staging of Shakespeare's play.

While acknowledging the force of Bentley's arguments, which rest primarily on possible acting-company management decisions, it also is helpful to be aware of their restricted focus. Other theatrical and staging influences upon Shakespeare beyond those of the public and private theatres need to be considered. In his seminal essay and in a later revision, Bentley did not mention in text or notes a key fact emphasized in this study: namely, that the only recorded early performances of *The Tempest*, in 1611 and then in 1613, were presented, not in private at Blackfriars or in public at the Globe, but before King James at Whitehall, where royal staging conventions prevailed.[2]

As previously noted, the King's Men had entertained so often in various capacities at court—some 15 recorded times in 1610 and some 22 times in 1611—that it can be reasonably assumed Shakespeare and other company members had a very professional knowledge of Whitehall stagecraft.[3] The stage and scenic references in *The Tempest* show evidence of having been composed by an author, most probably by Shakespeare himself, extremely conscious of the kind of Whitehall staging employed in royal entertainments, masques and pastoral dramas. Although it can be assumed that Shakespeare penned *The Tempest* anticipating at least some performances, though undocumented, at Blackfriars and probably also at the Globe, the playwright clearly created the work with its betrothal masque, possibly at royal command, with celebratory court production centrally in mind. While the relationship of *The Tempest* to staging in the public and private theatres has had no lack of commentators, the impact of the practical details of Whitehall stage techniques on Shakespeare's imagination still needs study. The actual and possible reflections of such techniques in the text of *The Tempest* represent another important critical index to the nature of the drama.

Certainty about the staging of *The Tempest* at court in Shakespeare's lifetime is not possible. Revels Office rolls show no large, special expenditures for a drama in 1611 and 1613, but surviving records naming *The Tempest* and other dramas by Shakespeare are incomplete. In recent years most commentators have assumed that *The Tempest* was produced at court as a traditional comedy on a relatively bare stage. Yet as a "spectacle" play presented in 1613 at a royal marriage, *The Tempest* would have "passed" at Whitehall as part pastoral and part masque and so may well have been mounted, as were other works at court in these genres, with at least some stage effects. Both John Long and A. M. Nagler have proposed this sort of possible elaborated court production;[4] and passages in the Folio text do suggest the utilization of those kinds of stage devices that the Revels Office could have put into service at little or no expense. Customary royal seating arrangements for a celebratory performance in the Banqueting House, it will be recalled, would place the king rear-center on a platform facing, first, an open, floor-level performing space at the center of the chamber, and then the uplifted stage at the hall's opposite narrow end, with the court spectators seated against the walls on "tiers" or "degrees" on three sides.[5] The play was obviously adaptable to different public and private stage spaces and conditions with only minor deviations from Folio stage directions and text; but the 1623 Folio, as printed, shows the drama particularly well suited to the "center-hall" and "raised-stage-with-machines" production techniques regularly employed at the Whitehall Banqueting House.[6] However the play may have been staged, the text clearly shows the influence of Whitehall seating arrangements and staging conventions on Shakespeare's creative imagination.

Consider how in scene 9 Prospero invites all present to inspect his own seat of state with their eyes.

> This Cell's my Court: heere haue I few attendants,
> And Subjects none abroad: pray you looke in.
>
> (D. 17)

Given the traditional center-stage placement at Whitehall of the main performer's "Court" or "seat" in relation to the commanding rear-center-hall placement of the king's royal court and throne, the gaze of the noble spectators would inevitably have been drawn first to the few attendants and humble stage seat of the Magus, and then by contrast to the richly dressed courtiers resting on stools next to the royal seat of James I. The platform holding the enthroned king, and also the attending seated aristocrats, would have been placed well away from the walls before a green carpet that covered the center-hall performing space. By Whitehall staging custom, the Cell and Court of Prospero would have been placed at the same height as the uplifted state seat of James I and his court at the hall's opposite end. Only from the king's seat would Prospero's Cell and the rest of the stage setting have been seen in perfect perspective.[7]

The play, then, would have unfolded between the seat of Prospero on stage and the contrasting seat of James in the hall proper, with action flowing forward and down from the stage to the central green-carpeted area in intimate proximity to the king and spectators. Steps leading from the stage to the carpeted area made close access to the monarch and spectators a simple matter; and under these intimate conditions, the appeal for prayers and understanding by the partially unmasked and actor-character Prospero in the epilogue could well have had stunning effect.

In act 3 Gonzalo, speaking of the wandering of the spiritually and physically lost nobles, uses the masquing terms "maze" and "trod."

> . . . here's a maze trod indeede
> Through fourth-rights, & Meanders
>
> (D. 13)

And in act 5 Alonso, awed upon meeting presumed dead seamen awakened from enchantments, sums up his wonder at all that he has experienced:

> This is as strange a Maze, as ere men trod,
> And there is in this businesse, more than nature
> Was euer conduct of
>
> (D. 18)

These references to a maze heavily "trod" rather than lightly paced, by corrupt figures moving in confused and wavering ways, suggest the kind of choreographed symbolic "maze" ballet movements made at court by performers on the central green carpet in the Banqueting House. "Then, as all actions of mankind/are but a Laborinth, or maze" sings the figure Daedalus in introducing dance as one of the "silent arts" in Ben Jonson's *Pleasure Reconciled to Virtue*; "So let your Daunces be entwin'd,/. . . As men may read each act you doo."[8] Jonson in the stage directions to *Hymenaei*, moreover, finds the symbolic silent art of the dancers so powerful he confesses that "it seemed to take away that Spirit from the Inuention, which the Inuention gaue to it: and left it doubtfull, whether the Formes flow'd more perfectly from the Authors braine, or their feete" (221, ll. 312–14).

The text of *The Tempest* further suggests that certain moving figures on the court stage, and in particular Prospero, at times would have appeared to glitter mysteriously in the dim light of the Whitehall chamber. Because the stage directions in scene 8 refer to Prospero's "*glistering apparell*" (D. 15), it is likely that this reference to the Magus's apparel, and to this same "*stolne Apparel*" worn "wet" by Trinculo and Stephano in scene 7 (D. 18), was imaginatively inspired by masque costumes that were traditionally sewn with the glistering metal "orbes" and "spangs." Ariel's masque-like air and water costumes, and even the "wet" outer garments of the "antic" Mariners in scene 2, may also have included wraps with "orbes" and "spangs" that would would have sparkled in oil or candlelight like shimmering reflections from water. Changeable, masque-inspired capes or weeds, easily slipped on over other costumes, allowed for quick and seemingly instantaneous transformations of appearance on stage, so that estimates by commentators of the time spans required for such changes, calculated in part by a count of lines, become relatively unimportant. As Andrew Gurr has pointed out, however, Ariel has 16 lines in which to change from air to water "weeds" in the play's second scene, the time span between Prospero's command "Go make thyselfe like to a Nymph o' th' Sea" and the stage direction "*Enter Ariel like a water-Nymph.*"[9] He apparently wears this water costume in following episodes through the end of scene 6, when in his "invisible" state he leads the comic conspirators off the stage to the music of tabor and pipe. He next has 71 lines, as Gurr has noted, to "don" another masque-like costume, the wings and attire of a Harpy, for his startling entrance during the banquet spectacle. After "*He vanishes in Thunder*" in the words of the stage directions, probably through a trap, he has either 38 or 71 lines to reappear without his Harpy weeds—depending on whether he comes onstage to hear Prospero say, "Bravely the figure of the Harpie hast thou/ Perform'd," or whether he remains offstage until the opening segment of scene eight (D. 13).

Shakespeare here transfers to the drama and gives new dimension to the masque device that was applied to Prospero: the "donning" and "doffing" of emblematic cloaks, hats, rainbow robes, or articles of costume to suggest symbolic changes in action and character. The convention is illustrated in the Prologue to Milton's *Comus* when the Attendant Spirit as a "glist'ring Guardian," in need of appearing in pastoral guise, takes off his "sky robes spun out of "Iris' Woof" and puts on "the Weeds and likeness of a Swain" to participate in the antimasque.[10] Later in the main masque, the Spirit, in introducing the main performers in Triumph to their noble parents, stands symbolically unmasked in his full identity as a heavenly messenger and protector.

Because in scene 8 of *The Tempest* Ariel confirms that he "presented Ceres," certain commentators, including Andrew Gurr who has again calculated time spans, assume that the Spirit also "donned" and "doffed" the Ceres costume and appeared in that role in the betrothal masque.[11] Yet Ariel had magically created the show at the request of and through the power of Prospero; the Spirit was, in court spectacle terminology and in fact, a "Presenter," and like the Attendant Spirit in *Comus*, distinguished from a performer playing a featured role. There is always the possibility at Blackfriars or the Globe that, if a limited number of actors were on call, Ariel might conceivably have "doubled" for Ceres out of practical necessity. But at court, professional musicians of the Kings Music, with long experience in descending from the heavens in their court-issued "sky robes," were available to speak, sing, compose music or play short roles should an acting company require assistance. Ariel would then simply have "presented" Ceres and left the role of the goddess to another performer.

The mysterious soft or *Solemne Musicke* called for throughout the Folio text appears an attempt to summon up sounds of the kind heard when fanciful magical episodes and spectacles of strangeness were staged at Whitehall. The sounds created a mood of mystery and, when needed during spectacle "discoveries," concealed the creaks and groans of court stage machines straining under heavy loads. Court musicians could readily have composed and performed such music for the royal presentations. Musicologist F. W. Sternfield, for example, has argued that the special, mood-inducing variety of "magic songs" required would have been suitable, not for a typical Blackfriars production, but for "masque-like scenes . . . presented at Court." In a complementary musical analysis, John Long maintains that court musicians, most likely Robert Johnson and one or more of nine other Whitehall musical performers, would have "joined forces with the King's Men for their royal performance." As Long observes, Johnson is believed to have composed the music for "Full Fathom Five" and "Where the Bee Sucks" for the 1613 performance.[12]

In harmony with the conjuring-variety stage illusions featured in court and in aristocratic productions are textual references in scene 7 to the disappearance, apparently through a "trap," of banquet food on a table that is carried on and off the stage. The magical banquet or magical "fare delicious" of sorcerers was a courtly theme introduced as early as 1581 in the French *Balet Comique* and repeated in Aurelian Townshend's masque *Tempe Restored* about Circe, William Browne's *The Inner Temple Masque* about Circe and Ulysses, and Milton's masque *Comus*, which features a "Juggler" or conjurer who, as the son of Circe, is also a genuine magician. In Shakespeare's play, a seventeenth century conjuring tabletop with a "trap" that slides open on its surface, such as that illustrated and described for a "decollation" trick in Reginald Scot's *The discouerie of witchcraft*, could have appropriately been used as a "property" of courtly theatre.[13]

In that part of the Folio text containing the betrothal masque which Prospero magically creates for Ferdinand and Miranda, the artfully choreographed entrance of Juno, an entrance that has stimulated much debate among critics, is yet one more episode that seems imaginatively composed under the influence of court staging conventions. Indeed, the episode was possibly included to accommodate the use of a special kind of stage machine readily available at Whitehall.

In scene 8 of the play, the controversial stage direction "*Juno descends*" appears on Folio page 14, in the right margin of the right column, opposite the line which ends with the rainbow goddess Iris referring to the absent Juno as "her soueraigne grace." Thirty lines later, after the very extended dialogue between Iris and the goddess Ceres, a statement by Ceres indicates that Juno has at last completed her descent and is pacing the performance space. "Great *Juno* comes," Ceres says, "I know her by her gate." The landing of Juno is confirmed when this goddess speaks next and, together with Ceres, begins the ritual of blessing the betrothed couple (D. 14).

On the asumption that the first published text of 1623 would conform in its details to production traditions at Blackfriars or the Globe, editors since the time of G. E. Bentley have usually eliminated or placed into footnotes the "Juno descends" stage direction on the grounds that it appears too early in the Folio text to be applicable to the very basic "descent methods" of those theatres. Alternative descent stage directions thought to be right for Blackfriars or the Globe are then inserted by editors at some later point or points, sometimes with editorial elaboration and, on occasion, even with staged heavenly "ascents" invented for Juno and Ceres. In such cases of editorial intervention, the different "descent" machines and techniques employed at court, as distinct from those of the public and private theatres, are usually either not mentioned or summarily dismissed, so that recent commentary generally leaves the impression that even at Whitehall, Juno's "descent" would be by the same means as that at Blackfriars or the Globe. John Jowett and Stanley Wells have rightly called the editorial treatment of this stage direction one the play's "most serious textual problems."[14]

At Blackfriars or the Globe where stage equipment in Shakespeare's period was limited, Juno would have been lowered—as would have Ariel if this spirit indeed "descended"—dangling at the end of a wire or more likely a rope from a fly gallery in a roof representing the heavens. Though commentators do not make the point, "dangling" descents were required because in the 1610–13 period, neither playhouse employed the fabric backflats or shutters needed to conceal sophisticated court-style levitation machines, and neither playhouse went to the expense of even attempting flight illusions of the sort regularly seen at court.

In their influential editions of the play, Stephen Orgel and Frank Kermode recognize that the first documented performance of *The Tempest* was presented at Whitehall, most probably in the Banqueting House, on "Hollowmas nyght" 1611, and that the second documented performance was again at Whitehall in 1613; and although they speculate about other possible productions, they realize that no other records of the play's production in Shakespeare's lifetime are extant. But Orgel takes exception to the view that the play, even in part, was written for court and produced like a masque." And both take the position, counter to that held by many scholars prior to Bentley, that *The Tempest* was best suited for the dangling-rope descents and basic stagecraft of the public and private theatres.[15] "If one accepts C. Walter Hodges's argument in *The Globe Restored*," writes Orgel, here relating imagined "flights" at court only to the "dangling-wire" methods ascribed by Hodges to the Globe, "public theatres may well have had flying machinery; whereas Inigo Jones had no such devices at court until his stage included a fly gallery in the 1630s. If, therefore, we wish to think of Ariel as entering flying at 3.3.52.2, he may have done so at the Blackfriars or the Globe, but not at court."[16]

Yet as evidence from Revels Office Rolls and masque documents in this study confirms, Whitehall stage effects were far more subtle than those in the public and private theatres. At Whitehall the changeable scenery, a fly gallery that in fact was in operation in the 1610–13 period, the regular appearance of masque apparitional figures of drama and fantasy, and the advanced "mechanics" of "descents" and "trapdoors," were of a kind remarkably well adapted to the spectacle episodes in *The Tempest*. My examination of Revels Office rolls reveals that seventeenth century wires were used to hold up light curtains and wooden frames, a fact suggesting the wires were fragile. Ropes, much stronger than the wires, were employed at Whitehall to lower and pull up the wooden struts supporting the heavy weight of human bodies on post-and-beam levitation machines. Only in public and private theatres were performers openly dangled from ropes and so crudely lowered and raised.

A hanging-on-a-rope descent, whether for Ariel or Juno, would not have been the "flight" method used on the Banqueting House stage, even if it were preferred—and it was not. In the words of Roger Warren, who reflects a dominant editorial and theatrical view, "to have Juno swaying about up there for nearly 30 lines" as the text requires, would be troublesome, for the dangling figure would be "likely to distract completely from the speeches, thus sacrificing any hope that the audience will get the point of the episode."[17] Scholars and editors, then, have inserted their own stage directions based on circular reasoning; they allege that the Folio direction is in the wrong place and, therefore, must be an addition from a "foul copy" or a late interpolation by scrivner Ralph Crane or by a hand other than Shakespeare's.[18] As Orgel has correctly observed, "editors have almost invariably assumed that the "*Juno descends*" reference "is misplaced, and belongs at line 102, when Ceres says 'Great Juno comes'" (175, n. 74.1). The need for speculation about "foul papers," and for further speculations on doubtful stylistic grounds, about a "second hand," largely dissipates when it is recognized that the play shows evidence of having been written by Shakespeare in considerable measure for the staging practices of the place where it was recorded to have been performed, that is, for production at Whitehall.[18]

Neglected in recent *Tempest* commentary is the fact that by 1606, for Ben Jonson's *Hymenaei*, Chief Architect

Inigo Jones was gracefully and astonishingly levitating large numbers of masquers together with luminous fabric clouds and chariots above the stage area of the Banqueting House—in a masque in which the three-dimensional "great globe" itself was seen revolving on stage—and he was doing so by the methods of magical illusionists on modern stages without the use of visible ropes or wires or other, crude, visible means of support. Jones, in association with the Revels Office, had decisively rejected the awkward, obvious, and low-budget dangling-on-a-rope descents, and he never used them to "float" persons to the Banqueting House stage. Ben Jonson himself, in his notes to *Hymenaei*, singled out Jones's levitation effects—involving performers riding on clouds that were seen to hover, "swell," "open," "stoupe," "fall gently downe upon the earth," and then to ascend—as causing "some rapture to the *beholders*."[19]

Juno's slow descent, during the recitation of 30 lines as recorded in the Folio text, is precisely in accord with staging practices utilized again and again at Whitehall in the period when *The Tempest* was presented there. The examination of the 17 Revels Office rolls covering the 1603–38 period shows that at court, curtains and shrouds were customarily hung from "wyres," probably of limited strength, that were in turn suspended from light frames placed out of the spectators sight above the stage; but that wooden beams mounted on or below the stage supported the "ropes" and "pulleys" used to lift and lower the very heavy weights involved in levitations.[20]

To arrange for the seemingly miraculous descent and suspension of Juno that takes place for a total of 30 lines, the Revels Office had only to bring into play the kind of machine regularly used at Whitehall by Jones following his study of court stagecraft in Italy. Such a suspension machine, placed behind backshutters and operated by ropes attached by pulleys to posts mounted at and below stage level, is depicted in John Webb's stage-section drawings of the set for William Davenant's masque *Salmacida Spoila* (1640), a set designed by Jones. The device was built to allow performers to sink down smoothly though a rear stage trap until they were completely out of sight. Directions for the construction of this type of suspension machine, and for a range of others related to it, appear in Nicola Sabbattini's famed Italian manual on stagecraft *Pratica Di Fabricar Scene.*[21]

According to Sabbattini, one or more vertical posts grooved about one-half foot deep over their length would be secured upright on the stage and concealed behind backflat scenery. A horizontal beam placed parallel to the backflats or backshutters—a beam cut to fit into and slide up and down in the vertical posts' grooves—would hold a seat for a performer who would be raised and lowered by ropes to simulate descents and ascents.

In some instances, the horizontal beam, when made to extend outward toward the audience through slits in the backflats instead of parallel to the backflats, would be fitted at its backstage end to a smaller piece of wood sliding up and down within the grooves of the supporting vertical post. At the horizontal beam's audience end, a performer would be suspended, seemingly in empty space, on an iron or wooden frame cradle hidden by an attached fabric cloud or other scenic device. Again, backstage ropes, secured by pulleys to the backstage upright post and then to the beam or perhaps to a ceiling support, would be used to haul the horizontal beam up and down, thus causing the suspended performer to seem to float down from or up to the theatrical heavens. "Stooping" or "sloping" descents such as those in *Hymenaei* could be arranged by hinging one end of the horizontal beam low on the backstage post, and then drawing the audience-end of the beam up and down in an arc using ropes attached by pulleys to a point on the beam about one quarter back from the audience end and next to the top of the vertical post. The ropes for the various levitation systems frequently ran down the posts to one of the understage winches turned by Revels Office stage workers.

As early as 1564, a Revels Office roll on performances in Windsor and Reading records the construction of an "iron woorke for A frame for A seate in A pageant," thus showing that by that date metal was used in the building of "frames" employed to seat performers on or above the stage.[22] Instructions by Sabbattini, moreover, include plans for a special cradle, with an attached extended stirrup for the performer's heel, that would allow the performer's body to hide the mechanism and so create the illusion of a figure moving in air apart from all nearby scenery.[23]

As suspensions at Whitehall grew ever more elaborate, groups of grooved posts, with horizontal beams extending between them or outward from them, would have been placed backstage to support clusters of up to six or eight masquers descending on a single cloud or scenic device. The increasingly sophisticated manipulation of ropes, together with the special hinging of the beams to sliding wooden supports, gradually produced a range of spectacular stage illusions: the "opening" of illumined cloud formations to allow for the central floating descents of one or more figures; and the movement of suspended performers, clouds, chariots and iconographic scenic devices back and forth over the stage, as well as up and down to and from the heavens. An examination of the official parchment Revels Office roll for 1611–12, listing expenditures beginning the end of October 1611 for stage properties, shows that payments were made for "Pullies," "Slyding ropes," "Raftboordes," and "Double plates"—all of which could have been utilized in the renovation or construction of lift machines.[24]

Court levitation methods appear to have stirred Shakespeare's "choreographic" imagination. In accord with Whitehall traditions of "choreographed" symbolic movement, the graceful descent of virtuous Juno appears in the Folio text to contrast with the harsh flight, described by Iris, of opposing lustful figures. As Juno floats down, Iris explains that libidinous Venus and her "waspish headed sonne," Cupid, are unable to cast a "wanton charme" because they were last seen far away "Cutting the clouds toward *Paphos*" (D. 14), that is, moving to earth in what would have been envisaged as a quick, sharp and graceless cloud descent appropriate to the pair's excessively passionate character.

Assuming a "descent" might again have been managed using a post-and-beam levitation machine, the only method employed at Whitehall, Juno, by contrast, would have been seen effortlessly descending to the middle heavens, next possibly hovering motionless above the stage, and then smoothly completing her descent and alighting on the stage proper. The movement would have been downward and outward; for by tradition "levitated" main masque performers alighted in the "upstage" or "back" position of the flat Renaissance stage, and, to the masquing cue-word "come," eventually paced across the stage and down steps leading to a green-carpeted area in the center of the hall, there to join with other featured performers in complementing nobles or royalty "seated in state" and then in "taking out" spectators in a revel of dancing.[25]

Such customary action is in part suggested in the betrothal masque when Iris, in the name of Juno "The Queene o'th skie," bids Ceres to leave her usual haunts and "Here on this grasse-plot, in this very place,/To come, and sport" (D. 14). At Whitehall the "grasse-plot, in this very place" would appear to signify, beyond a delightful rural lawn, the green carpet in the hall proper; and the term "sport," the capers and dancing of the main performers in the anticipated betrothal masque revels.[26] The graceful, choreographed pacing forward of Juno following her descent, symbolic of her virtue, would occur when Ceres utters the cue words, "Great *Juno* comes, I know her by her gate" (D. 14).

In *The Tempest*, the main masquers Ceres, Iris and Juno are never allowed to "sport" in customary, harmonious main masque revels dances. Instead, as the goddesses watch the ending of preliminary rustic dances by Nymphs and Reapers that traditionally came before the graceful main dances by the featured figures, the magician-creator of the masque, Prospero, "starts sodainly and speakes, after which to a strange hollow and confused noyse, they heauily vanish."

The masque is thus interrupted before the main masque dances take place. The Magus speaks of a sudden change in his thoughts, of how he had "forgot" the sedition of Caliban. It is here that the broken-off spectacle serves as an external symbol of the breach in Prospero's mind and imagination. The Magus announces that the masque is an enactment, not of his reason, but of his "present fancies"—notably fancies of ideal harmony as distinguished from fancies of fury projected by Prospero in antic spectacles enacted earlier in act 4 (D. 15). With the "heavy" vanish of the masque figures, the internal conflicts of the enchanter together with the base "fabric" of the masque production are exposed.

This odd disappearance, with the heaviness of the vanish calling attention to weight, may well have its origins in the operation and malfunctioning of court stage traps and lift machines. Only four years before *The Tempest* was first presented at Whitehall in 1611, an understage lift machine malfunctioned during the main masque of Campion's *Lord Hayes Masque* (1607), destroying the ideal entrance of the main masquers, who rose on traps from among opening scenic trees, in the guise of Knights of Apollo. Stage directions describe the entrance as it was supposed to take place. Nine trees, three by three, were made "to sinke, and this was effected by an Ingin plac't under the stage." After the trees mechanically "cleft in three parts, and the Masquers appeared out of the tops of them, the trees were sodainly conuayed away, and the first three Maskers were raysed againe by the Ingin."

A marginal note alongside the directions, however, blames "the simplicity, negligence, or conspiracy of the painter" for leaving the mechanism of the trees "unset," "the patterne of them the same day hauing been shown with much admiration." On the evening of performance, the note continues, "the passing away of the trees was somewhat hazarded." This kind of malfunction could have been enormously distracting, since the trees appear to have been "passing away"—perhaps in fits and starts—just as the masquers would have been bowing and so making an "honour to the King" seated in state.[27]

James Shirley in his masque *The Triumph of Peace* (1634) went so far as to include a stage-engine failure as a structural feature of his work.[28] Although Shirley wrote his masque some years after the court productions of *The Tempest,* this, considered together with the actual lift-and-descent machine failure in 1607 in *Lord Hayes Masque,* points to the kind of stage machine difficulties that could occur during this period when, beginning with *Hymenaei,* ever greater numbers of persons were being raised and lowered on wooden post-and-beam stage mechanisms.

Sounds also suggest scenic devices in use. The very recognizable "strange, hollow . . . noyse" that disrupts the betrothal masque in *The Tempest* is one that accompanies the operation of large, rumbling horizontal-beam and vertical post stage lift and descent machines overweighted with players or scenery. In *The Tempest* the "written in" sound would suggest that of an overloaded, reverberating post-and-beam machine affecting the "heavy" vanish of performers possibly on a platform or on seats sliding down through an opening in the stage. In Shirley's masque the noise of a breaking machine is accompanied by "a confusion . . . within"; the "heavy" vanish in *The Tempest* is said to be "confused" by the "noyse" that is both "strange" and "hollow." The ungainly nature of this "heavy" vanish becomes evident when compared to Milton's allusion in the "Nativity Ode" to the proper "sliding" operation of a descent machine. In the poem, the figure Peace appears "*softly* sliding/Down through the turning sphere" amid "the amorous clouds dividing" (italics added).[29]

The hollow noise alluded to in *The Tempest* still can be heard on occasion on modern stages, above the strains of "covering" musical crescendos, to the distress of contemporary performers presenting otherwise flawless levitation illusions using reverberating mechanisms that are but variants of the early post-and-beam suspension machines of the Revels Office. The secret of the post-and-beam "lift" and "levitation" devices was rediscovered and elaborated on in the nineteenth century by illusionists John Nevil Maskelyne, George Alfred Cooke and David Devant at Egyptian Hall and St. Michael's Hall, London. Their "floating" of persons in the air, together with their original methods of passing solid metal hoops entirely around figures suspended by the old post-and-beam means, represented an advance in levitation illusion "technology" but also a handing down to modern designers of an old but very effective Renaissance stage effect.[30]

In *The Tempest*, Shakespeare's apparent references to Whitehall-type stage machines, costumes and choreography are accompanied by references to Whitehall-type scenic effects. In writing Prospero's famous speech, which makes the masque a metaphor for the ephemeral life of human beings, Shakespeare is clearly alluding to reminiscences of visionary scenes designed by Inigo Jones that had been presented on the Whitehall stage.

"No tongue: all eyes: be silent," the Magus commands at the beginning of the betrothal masque as "*Soft musick*" plays (D. 14). After the masque is broken off, the Magus in a brief reverie captures, in the manner of Ben Jonson in his nostalgic notes to his early masques, the sad dreamlike transience of life and of court theatrical art.

> Our Reuels now are ended: These are actors,
> (As I foretold you) were all Spirits, and
> Are melted into Ayre, into thin Ayre,
> And like the baselesse fabricke of this vision
> The Clowd-capt Towers, the gorgeous Palaces,
> The solemne Temples, the great Globe itselfe,
> Yea, all which it inherit, shall dissolue,
> And like this insubstantiall Pageant faded,
> Leave not a racke behinde: we are such stuffe
> As dreames are made on; and our little life
> Is rounded with a sleepe.
>
> (D. 15)

Just as Jonson alluded in *Hymenaei* to performers "dissoluing" or as "dissolu'd" (ll. 433, 340) on stage, so too

Shakespeare, referring here both to "actors" and to the wooden racks used to stretch and hold fabric scenery, alludes to the melting and fading of stage figures and scenes. The stage magic of the first great English stage-design illusionist, Inigo Jones, has here cast its spell, successfully conveying the sense that figures and scenes did at times miraculously "dissolve" into nothingness. Such was the theatrical experience achieved by Jones, as explained by Sabbattini: upstage wing and back flats were suddenly changed or figures quickly lowered on traps at the very moment audience attention was misdirected to down stage or central hall areas by the planned actions of players, musicians, or spectator accomplices.[31] The blurring of the audience's senses through misdirection, and through a resulting delayed reaction to upstage changes, indeed caused spectators to believe that they had witnessed seemingly amazing "dissolutions," "disappearances," and transformations. Although Jones's stage art has been carefully studied, the magical effect of stage "wonders" such as these still deserves notice and appreciation.

For those noble spectators at Whitehall, who along with the king and queen, witnessed or performed in masque after masque, Prospero's speech would doubtless have stirred memories of splendid "cloud-capp'd towers" like the tower of the Palace of Fame, surmounted by Fame with her head "in the Cloudes" (305, l. 454), in the *Masque of Queenes* (1609); the "gorgeous palaces,/ The solemn temples" like the Palace of Oberon, with its transparent walls and gates, that appeared from a great rock in *Oberon: The Faery Prince* 1611, or the Palace of Fame in *Queenes*, or the Temple of Peace in *The Vision of the 12. Goddesses* (1604), or the palace with columns of burnished gold in *Tethys Festival* (1610).

The Magus's embracing and climactic reminiscence of the "great globe itself" would, for court spectators, have brought to memory *Hymenaei* (1606) with its huge silver sphere of the earth holding eight main masquers artfully turning at the rear center of the stage. In *The Haddington Masque* (1608) the globe, again revolving with the featured masquers inside, reappeared when a cliff surrounded by trees opened. This last set was apparently redesigned for the masque *Oberon*, presented on 1 January 1611. With some possible repainting, the set could have been employed again ten months later to serve in the first Whitehall production of *The Tempest*, with the pulling or closing of backflats alternately disclosing or concealing an upstage cave-like Cell at the center of the scene.

The issue of the "descent" of Juno in *The Tempest* remains a fascinating element in the analysis of possible early staging; as it has been noted, the goddess could not have floated smoothly and slowly down, with a likely stop to hover in space, by established Whitehall stage-machine methods without the existence of a backflat to conceal the levitation machine—in this instance perhaps a conventional but repainted scene showing a rural "island" with a "cell" at its center. If this scene were used, then it is remotely possible that to open the play, the Revels Office might also have used one other scene: a repainted seascape that would have been "discovered" on a darkened stage to lighting and thunder effects.[32]

Masque writer James Shirley, in his play *Loves Crueltie. A Tragedy* (1640), includes a reminiscence by the character Hippolito about the "wonder" and "rapture" of a court tempest-at-sea scene containing stage effects very much like those at the beginning of *The Tempest*. Hippolito remarks that during the performance of an unnamed court masque by the "immortal English *Jonson*," there appeared on stage amid "waues capering about tall ships" "a tempest so artificiall and suddaine in the clouds, with a generall darkenes and thunder so seeming made to threaten, that you would cry out with the Marriners in the works, you cannot ícape drowning."[33] This description, which includes allusions to Arion and the Tritons, is not applicable to any known masque or other work by Jonson. But in key respects it might be an allusion to scene one of Shakespeare's play in which, to claps of thunder, Mariners give themselves up to drowning and shout, "All lost, to prayers, to prayers, all lost!" (D. 1). Was Shirley imaginatively improvising or confused—or might the Revels Office have arranged a Whitehall staging, with scenic "fabric" and storm effects, for the opening scene of Shakespeare's play?

Given the special qualities of this unique drama, with its Magus protagonist and action turning on magic; its pastoral yet masque-like iconographic cosmic setting; its inclusion of Jonsonian-type spectacles of strangeness; its incorporation of the traditional stately court "descent" of a goddess from the theatrical heavens in a masque within the play; its spectacle structure and individualized courtly character-types; its apparent allusions to masque-style music and choreographic movement; and its evocation of life's transience through reference to known court scenic "fabrics," the Revels Office would almost certainly have regarded *The Tempest* as a special pastoral dramatic spectacle, with courtly elements, deserving the use of a levitation machine and probably other stage effects as well.

However early court performances of *The Tempest* were actually mounted, the play, as printed in the Folio edition, bears the imaginative mark of a work written under the impact of Whitehall stage effects and theatrical conventions. Court theatrical taste had been evolving in the early part of the century, with dispersed-scenery productions giving way to increasingly varied onstage machines and to changing, multiple, full-stage scenes framed within a proscenium arch. *The Tempest's* text and stage directions, though composed to be open to private and even to public theatre presentation, most directly, if modestly, reflected the courtly fascination with masque-like dramatic spectacle. *The Tempest* also anticipated the general audience demand in the late seventeenth century for public-theatre "heroic dramas" stressing music, song, choreographic movements and exotic settings capable of being mounted against full-stage scenic flats. All these elements were drawn together by Shakespeare in *The Tempest* to surprise his audience with delight and fear and to cast in new symbolic shadings, theatrical and literary representations of a longed-for Golden Age.

9. *An Indian torchbearer costume by Inigo Jones for the* Masque of the Middle Temple and Lincoln's Inn *(1613). Designs for the heroic main masquers playing Virginia Indians are not extant.*

Jones in his costume-design iconography does not appear visually to associate an "ethnic" New World native with a nonhuman "Other" figure, the Earthly Spirit. Critics have suggested, however, that Shakespeare under the influence of contemporaneous writings and illustrations reflected a demonized New World native in the representation of Caliban as a supposed type of the earthly, monstrous "Other."

Devonshire Collection, Chatsworth.
By permission of the Chatsworth Settlement Trustees.
Courtesy of the Courtauld Institute of Art.

10. *Model of the hall at Whitehall, disclosing the stage and seating arrangements for the pastoral drama* Florimène, *constructed from Inigo Jones's ground plan. View from above showing the chair of state (bottom center) on a raised platform facing the stage.*

By permission of the Globe Education Center, Southwark, England. Photograph by the author.

11. *Side view of the model disclosing the hall arrangements for* Florimène.

By permission of the Globe Education Center, Southwark, England. Photograph by the author.

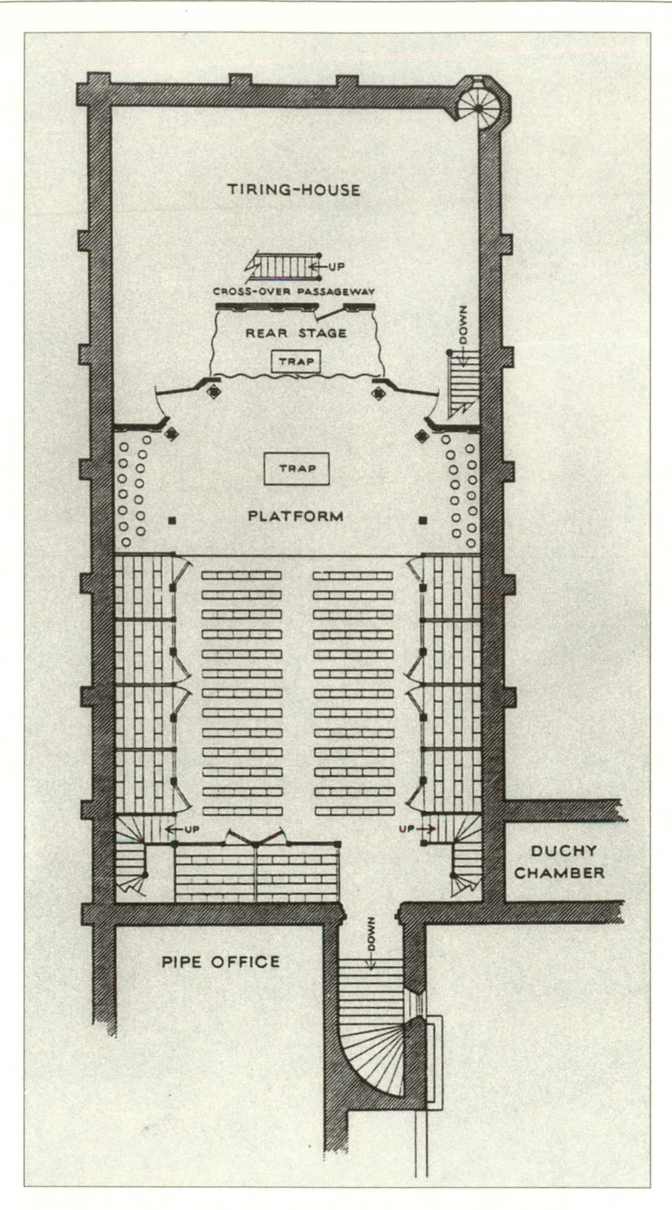

12. *Floor plan of Blackfriars indoor playhouse in a modern reconstruction based on early documents.*

From Irwin Smith's Blackfriars Playhouse.
By permission of New York University Press.

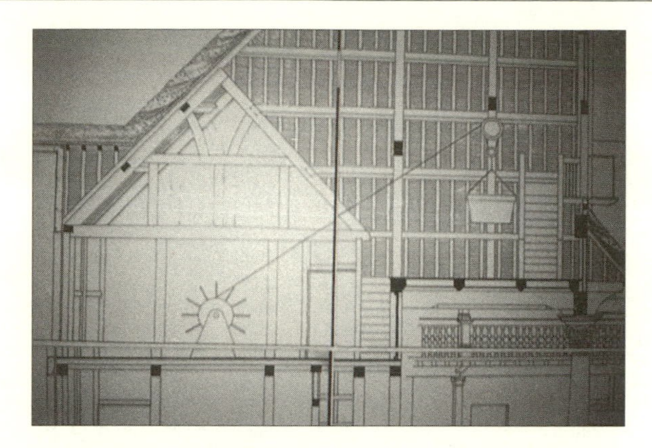

13. *Design showing a modern reconstruction of a crude public theatre "descent machine," the sort used in Shakespeare's period at Blackfriars and the Globe. Such a machine lowered figures to the stage at the end of a hanging, exposed rope that, beyond the view of the audience, ran up through a pulley (upper right) and then across to a controlling windlass (left of center. John Pory, in a January 1606 letter, castigated this type of "stale downright perpendicular" descent, "like a bucket into a well," in offering praise for the contrasting court descents of main masque figures in* Hymenaei *who came "gently sloping down."*

By permission of the Shakespeare's Globe Trust.
Photograph by the author.

14. *A bower employed to frame performers amid wooded hillsides in Inigo Jones's design for William Daavenant's masque* Salmacida Spoilia *(1640) presented at Whitehall.*

Devonshire Collection, Chatsworth.
By permission of the Chatsworth Settlement Trustees.
Courtesy of the Courtauld Institute or Art.

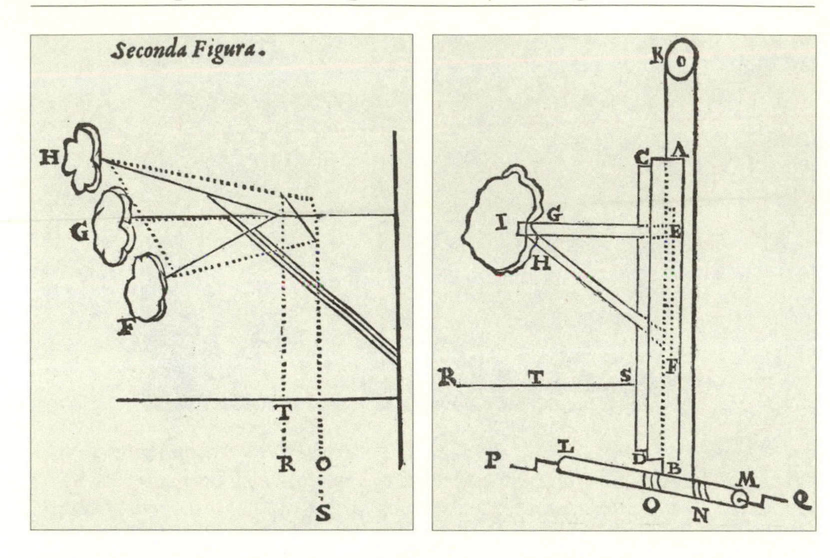

15. *Diagrams from Nicola Sabbatini's* Pratica di Fabricar Scene *showing stage machines for the levitation of persons and clouds on the courtly stage. The diagrams make clear how in* The Tempest *Juno, the "Queene of the Skie," could very slowly and lightly "descend" from the Whitehall theatrical heavens without "cutting the clouds" in a crude, hasty descent, and without being let down dangling from a rope.*

Left: one or more suspension beams, hinged at the rear to hidden backstage posts and operated by ropes so as to swing in an arc in front, lower and raise scenic devices and figures in the forward-stage area.

Right: A more complex machine employs a horizontal suspension beam that extends forward over the stage toward the audience; it is pulled vertically with ropes at the rear within grooves in concealed, backstage posts.

Court machines of these kinds were studied by Inigo Jones in Italy and then imitated by him to produce elaborate cloud and "descent" effects at Whitehall.

By permission of the Henry E. Huntington Library.

16. *Masque-like, full-stage Restoration scenic designs for Settle's heroic drama* The Empress of Morocco *staged in 1673 in Dorset Garden Theatre. Designs of this sort were also introduced into Blackfriars Theatre toward the end of the seventeenth century many years after Shakespeare's death. The designs no longer featured the sweeping, moving cosmic iconography of the Jacobean Whitehall stage which showed the earth and heavens, but rather were more limited in scenic effect and imbued with a new verisimilitude.*

By permission of the British Library.

17. *Jacques Callet's etching of a typical French grand ballet "entry," this one introducing a combat at barriers, in Paris, 1627.*

From the collection of the Bibliotheque Nationale (Ob 1627), Coll. Herrin no^t 2105

Four

The New Theatrical Hieroglyphics

In those years just before and after *The Tempest* was composed and twice presented at court, certain seventeenth century "moderne" theatrical writers spoke out emphatically against the tyranny of an exclusive reliance upon classical themes and images. These were revisionist authors of court masques, writers who partly rejected the classicism of Ben Jonson and who sought to produce new imaginative works suitable for specific social occasions and known individual performers. These authors favored original inventions, unique images and literary components functioning in harmony with a novel hinge, and they defined the kind of theatrical work to which Shakespeare gave expression in *The Tempest*.

Shakespeare's play interweaves traditional classical types and allusions with new Renaissance theatrical materials and forms. References to Dido and Carthage in the play's third sequential scene; the appearance of Ariel like a harpy in scene 7; and the wide emphasis upon themes of "storm" and "wandering" echo motifs in Virgil's *Aeneid*.[1] The familiar goddesses in the betrothal masque in scene 8 are immediately identifiable as classical types of the sort carried over from masque to masque by Inigo Jones and Jonson in works such as *Hymenaei* (1606), *The Haddington Masque* (1608) and *Love freed from Ignorance* (1611).[2] And vestiges of a classical Latin play structure can be seen within a singular spectacle-triumph dramatic design. Just as the original form of the *The Tempest* shows the influence of different theatrical and literary genres in transition, so too the content of the play reflects revisionist theatrical practices and theories that give priority to fancy over reason and that stress unique symbolism, different from those governing the classically constrained and rationally controlled works of Ben Jonson.

The betrothal masque was an enactment, after all, of Prospero's "present fancies," fancies of "virtue" that contrasted with the fancies of "furie" represented in antic spectacles (D. 14–15). Insofar as *The Tempest* is a Renaissance play with Latin play derivations, such fancies, in harmony or tension with reason, are "acted out" directly by the protagonists through speeches and encounters fostering dramatic conflict. But insofar as *The Tempest* is a masque-like drama, the fancies themselves are objectified in the iconographic spectacles which serve as partial revelations of the motivations and desires of the central figures.

As early as 1604, in the Preface to *The Vision of the 12. Goddesses*, Samuel Daniel pointed out that the "Shewes" at court were especially dependent upon the original "intentions" of the authors. The shows were seen to point to the evanescent imaginative, affective, and dream life of figures, this inner dream life often at variance with waking action and frequently exposing inner "error":

> in such matters of Shewes these like Characters (in what forme soeuer they be drawne) serue vs but to read the intention of what wee would represent: . . . for that these apparitions and shewes are but as imaginations, and dreames that

> portend our affections, and dreams are neuer in all points agreeing right with waking actions; and therefore were they aptest to shadow whatsoeuer error might bee herein presented.[3]

Through external dream-iconography the "Shewes" thus represented the disordered inner "affections" of man as a microcosm, affections believed to correspond to and influence the elements of the earth and universe—the wider macrocosm. In contrast to the disordered theatrical dream world of antic *intermezzo* sequences in masques, the main masque dream world contained ideal, if insubstantial, visions of harmony and delight. The names of even some of Jonson's masques—masques with strong neoclassical elements—capture this ideal imaginative realm: *Oberon, The Faery Prince* (1611), *Love Restored* (1616), *The Vision of Delight* (1617) and *Pleasure reconciled to Virtue* (1618).

The need of court writers to compose on command for particular social occasions and particular masque performers, often in a particular indoor or outdoor setting, spurred the invention of original "hinges" and hieroglyphics. Under these pressures and constraints, reformist authors, moving beyond Jonson's neoclassicism, frequently altered or even abandoned classical conventions and characters. In accommodating their materials to social and practical requirements, they produced artistic works that were indeed new. "And though these images haue often times diuers significations," declares Daniel in the introduction to *The Vision of the 12. Goddesses*, "we tooke them only to serue as Hierogliphicqs for our present intention, according to some properly that fitted our occasion. . . ." So muddled and contradictory are the mythographers' interpretations of hieroglyphics, Daniel argues, that he simply ignores them. By contrast, Ben Jonson generally stressed the precise, traditional meaning of classical "Hierogliphicqs" and characters in his early masques and in his tragedies *Sejanus* and *Catiline* by appending notes with citations and explanations of classical sources. Taking a different position, Daniel maintains that he will use the "Hierogliphicqs"

> without obseruing other their misticall interpretations, wherein the Authors themselues are so irrigular & confused, as the best Mytherologers, who wil make somewhat to seem any thing, and so unfaithful to themselues, as they haue left vs no certain way at all, but a tract of confusion to take our course at aduenture. And therfore owing no homage to their intricate obseruations, we were left at libertie to take no other knowledge of them, then fitted our present purpose . . . then they fell out to stand with the nature of the matter in hand.

"Modernist" Thomas Campion, in the introduction to *Somerset's Masque* (1613), went so far as to claim that in what he called "our days," conventional iconographic figures, though of some "use," were no longer appropriate to the new inventive purposes of the writer. Campion, possibly even holding a copy of *The Tempest* "in hand," argued that modern fictions needed to feature new imaginative figures of power.

> In ancient times, when any man sought to shadowe or heighten his Inuention, he had store of seyned persons readie for his purpose As *Saatyres, Nymphes &* their like: such were then in request and beliefe among the vulgar. But in our dayes, although they haue not vtterly lost their vse, yet finde they so litle credit, that our moderne writers haue rather transferd their fictions to the persons of Enchaunters & Commaunders of Spirits, as that excellent Poet *Torquato Tasso* hath done, and many others.
>
> In imitation of them (having a presentation in hand for Persons of high State) I grounded my whole Inuention vpon Inchauntmens and severall transformations.[4]

In his introduction to *Tethys Festival* (1610), Samuel Daniel went further in urging writers to break with the "tyrannie" of classical conventions and to freely create original images in harmony with their inventions:

> And for these figures of mine, if they come so drawn in all proportions to the life of antiquity (from whose tyrannie, I see no reason why we may not emancipate our inuentions, and be as free as they, to vse our owne images) yet I know them such as were proper to the busines, and discharged those parts for which they serued, with as good correspondencie, as our appointed limitations would permit.[5]

But the new freedom Daniel felt as a creator of masques, unlike that Shakespeare felt as a playwright, was curtailed in performance by the authority of the court architect. Daniel meekly deferred in politic fashion to the artistic "tyrannie" of Inigo Jones over the details of the actual, performed show.

> But in these things werein the onely life consists in shew; the arte and inuention of the Architect giues the greatest grace, and is of most importance: ours, the least part of least note in the time of the performance thereof, and therefore haue I interserted the discription of the artificiall part which only speakes M. Inigo Jones. (E 2)

The theatrical outlook advanced by Thomas Campion and Samuel Daniel, to which Shakespeare in *The Tempest* was deeply indebted, stressed novel inventions and openly suggestive imaginative iconography, which allowed the fancy of the poet to create original shows and character-types. Shakespeare's general movement away from the Jonsonian masque iconographic tradition, centered on classical or conventional "hieroglyphics" with established meanings, has made *The Tempest* a critically obscure but profoundly suggestive work. The classical allusions and echoes that do appear throughout the play—such as those in the betrothal masque with established meanings—are ultimately subsumed by the wider "moderne" masque-like symbolism of the magical island; the tempestuous storm; the mysterious "maze" in which enchanted nobles wander; the overall strangeness of the apparitions, spirits and visionary shows; and the suggestiveness of the powerful and controlling Magus himself with his "*glistering apparell*" (D. 13).

Consequently, the long history of attempts to uncover definitive, specific references to ideas or historical persons in the drama's vague and evocative symbolism has hardly produced agreement. O. J. Campbell stated as early as 1870 that Prospero signifies Shakespeare; and Prospero's magic, dramatic art. Advancing an early allegorical reading, James Russell Lowell in 1870 thought that Prospero stood for true Imagination, Ariel for Fancy, and Caliban for Brute Understanding. Colin Still in 1927 argued that Prospero was a type for the magician Dr. John Dee. But Glynne Wickham claimed that Prospero figured King James, the enemy of magicians. Recently, Michael Srigley maintained that the Magus signified the occultist Rudolph II, the Holy Roman Emperor. My own addition to this list—made without any conviction that the play's symbolism offers specific and conclusive support—is that Prospero could reflect, among others, the sometimes flinty and arbitrary Court Architect Inigo Jones who, out of the fabric of his theatrical art, created visionary stage spectacles that caused wonder in performance and then faded from memory.

As for other characters in the play, a British National Theatre production by Peter Hall in 1975 presented Juno as Queen Elizabeth; but Wickham maintained that it is Iris who signifies Queen Elizabeth, that Juno signifies Queen Anne, and that Miranda signifies Princess Elizabeth. In 1875 Edward Dowden said that Ferdinand was a type for John Fletcher; but a host of later critics found Ferdinand to represent the prospective bridegroom of Princess Elizabeth; that is, either Frederick, the Elector Palatine; or, in 1611, possibly Phillip of Spain. Scrigley thought that Ferdinand signified the ideal Hermetic Monarch about to usher in a Golden Age, and that Miranda figured the goddess Persephone.[6]

Some of these designations are better than others. For example, the general metaphoric identification of Prospero's magic with the illusions of both the theatrical arts and Shakespeare's dramatic art, an identification applicable throughout the drama, is rightly appealing.[7] All the designations described above fit one or more selected passages in the play, although with varying levels of probability, and a number can be related in interesting combinations. But the nuances and contexts of the drama, when read in its entirety, result in problems for all those interpretations seeking to identify one single character throughout the play exclusively with one single historical person or abstract idea. Of course, the symbolic "unmaskings" staged by Shakespeare in *The Tempest* clearly point to the underlying human identities of characters as they appear in the world of the drama. The Magus as a character, however, proves something of anomaly because in the Epilogue, in the manner of Puck at the conclusion of *A Midsummer Night's Dream*, Prospero further "unmasks" to show himself an actor appealing directly to a court audience.

The often unsettling, eerie, chimerical spectacles point to disturbing disjunctions in the political and social world of the play,[8] and given the passing and shadowy possible associations of characters with living persons, vaguely point to political and social dislocations in the actual world beyond. But because the spectacles also objectify some of the inner fancies, desires and compulsions of the characters within the drama, the values and inner motivations of these characters are dramatically acted out only to a degree. As a result, a character such as Prospero can be seen to be partly a dimensional human figure, partly a "Magus" archetype, and ultimately a symbolic creation. Prospero gives relatively limited emotional, acted-out human expression to his deepest inner life, to his stated "fury" at the treason of his enemies, and to his obviously profound imaginative delight at the impending bounteous marriage of Ferdinand and Miranda. Instead, he fancifully projects his unrestrained anger and his idealized hopes for the marriage into the original but formalized action and iconography of the spectacles of strangeness and, in doing so, reveals his desires and feelings in both typal and symbolic ways.

The Magus thus emerges as a representation of that new

kind of magical "moderne" theatrical figure praised by Campion in his preface to *Somerset's Masque*, an enchanter and commander of spirits who replaced formally defined classical types. The two antic, elemental attendants of Prospero—the airy spirit Ariel, and the lumbering Caliban whom Prospero calls "Thou Earth" (D. 4)—accordingly emerge as newly minted, partially individualized theatrical figures, still somewhat derived from formal typal patterns.[9] Although Caliban has been seen to mirror New World natives, including the noble savages of Michel de Montaigne's famed essay "Des Cannibales," the humanized monster has also rightly been found to have affinities with the threatening, partly human, partly monstrous beings of the largely fictitious late medieval travel volume *The Book of Sir John Maundeville* (c. 1322), a work recounting strange wonders that was published in many editions throughout the sixteenth century and contained in Samuel Purchas's *Hakluytus Posthumus or Purchas his Pilgrimes* (1625). Yet, as a composite symbolic representation, Caliban both reflects and transcends such explicit types.

In Shakespeare's structured employment of contending ordering and antic figures, the playwright highlighted the stark difference between "uncivilized Caliban"—a pivotal antic and, at times, sympathetic figure, but by no means the work's hero—and the "lettered," aged, caustic, manipulative, and finally well-intentioned commander of spirits. Caliban, somewhat like the antic but very different Bottom of *A Midsummer Night's Dream*, appears as the "low" but dreaming figure who, through contrast, gives dimension to the ideal projected fancies and visions, and to the imperfect realities experienced by the other characters.

Reflecting shadowy symbolism and some practices of masques, the visionary shows in *The Tempest*, by presenting the fancies that end in jolting awakenings to actual life, give final configuration to themes long present in Shakespearean drama. It will be remembered that in earlier years in *Romeo and Juliet* such imaginative dream life is mocked by Mercutio as the product of "vaine phantasie,/Which is as thin of substance as the ayre,/And more inconstant then the wind" (D. 57). In *A Midsummer Night's Dream*, a play giving seeming objective reality to dream-like events and figures, the soldier-ruler Theseus similarly derides the reveries of lovers and the creations of poets as the "tricks" of "strong imagination":

> That, if it would but apprehend some ioy,
> It comprehends some bringer of that joy,
> Or in the night, imagining some feare,
> How easie is a bush suppos'd a Bear?
>
> (D. 159)

Yet "strong imagination" is forcefully if somewhat mysteriously defended by Theseus' future bride, the Amazon Hippolyta. She declares that, when imaginative stories are witnessed by persons with "minds transfigured," then from this transforming experience there "growes something of great constancie" (D. 159).

In *The Tempest*, Shakespeare, in accord with the views and practices of "modernist" court theatrical writers, employed such strong imagination to forge original and often dream-like hieroglyphics that point with extraordinary emotive and suggestive power to "constants" in mortal life.

FIVE

On the Symbolism of The Tempest

A profound and continuing wonder stirred in characters by visionary dreams, reveries and magical spectacles is at the deepest core of *The Tempest*. This deep experience of wonder, which transforms corrupt characters and inspires the virtuous, distinguishes this late masque-like drama from comedies and tragedies more dependent upon traditional, unfolding, confrontational dramatic conflict.

"O, it is monstrous: monstrous:" calls out the terrified Alonso upon seeing Ariel disguised as a Harpy. The man of "sin," Alonso stands transfixed as his more insightful companion Gonzalo says, "I' th name of something holy, Sir, why stand you/In this strange stare?" (D. 13).

"Let me liue here euer," Ferdinand joyfully remarks upon seeing the visionary betrothal masque, "So rare a wondered Father and a wise/Makes this place Paradise" (D. 15).

"These are not naturall euents, they strengthen/From strange to stranger," says Alonso in awe when meeting seamen whom he thought dead (D. 18).

In the final scene Gonzalo conveys some sense of the total experience of the island's magic and the strange events that have gone before:

> All torment, trouble, wonder, and amazement
> Inhabits heere. Some heauenly power guide vs
>
> (D. 17)

The narrative contains relatively little action, but those characters who wander, dream, stare and listen in awestruck horror or amazement are changed and metaphorically reborn through the strangeness of things experienced but rarely understood. In this way, fancies and symbolic magical spectacles underlie and in large measure motivate action. Thematically, the play moves from a range of subjective and fanciful utopian reveries and visions interspersed, as has been seen, with jolting and equally fanciful "antic" countervailing spectacles, on to a revelation of true identities and of external reality.

Contrasting virtuous and corrupted dreams of a Golden Age, a coming millennium, haunt the imaginations of central characters. In the manner of a host of utopian and millenarian writers of the late Renaissance, the characters speculate, with differing degrees of casualness, seriousness, selfishness, or moral rectitude, on some personal variant of an ideal future time, a period when their sometimes wildly imaginative reveries on power, wealth, possessions, or natural plentitude may be fulfilled. External "reality" is placed in ever-changing perspectives as it is cast against the characters' imagined visions, and these visions are constantly tested against that reality.

The idle, irresponsible fancies of Gonzalo on the creation of an ideal commonwealth; the vicious speculations of Caliban, Trinculo and Stephano on riches and rule gained by murder; the parallel brutal, thwarted reveries and acts of Sebastian and Alonso aimed at seizing political power also through murder; and the ideal dreams of Prospero on fecundity and blessedness in marriage—all are presented through spectacle imagery and allusion. But in each case the reveries projected in spectacle, whether good or ill, are shattered or qualified by a rational awakening to earthly realities. Thematically, the play is a sharp but not cynical corrective to then-prevalent dreams of a Golden Age or a "new world" of perfect harmony, dreams given theatrical form in the main masques of court spectacles and suggested too, in very different ways, in the fictions of both utopian literature and the literature of exploration.

As symbolically represented by unique characters and action on a magical Mediterranean island, this awakening to earthly realities—to deceit and moral ambiguity in politics and social life and, in the case of Prospero, to the fact of human mortality—has been observed to contain oblique reflections of the "brave" new, but troubled, colonial world. Yet the drama's varied political, social and religious motifs are absorbed within a sweeping symbolism suggesting that all imagined ideal societies—whether those that might exist in some "brave new world" of total innocence, or those seriously or mockingly envisaged in the dreamlike fantasy of utopian literature, or those wondrously represented in the fleeting Golden Age theatrical Triumphs of aristocrats—all are uniformly subject to the coils of an imperfect, mortal social life.

Before *The Tempest* was first staged in 1611, the ideal aristocratic social visions that climaxed court masquing spectacles, though diverse in their "hinges," were notable in not directly representing the New World or colonial enterprises. When the New World finally did make its appearance on the Whitehall stage in a masque presented on 15 February 1613, the year of the second and last recorded performance of Shakespeare's play, this New World proved yet another fantastical variation of that golden world carried over from masque to masque. George Chapman's *The Memorable Maske of the two Honorable Houses of Inns of Court: the Middle Temple and Lyncolns Inne* featuring twelve Virginian Indians as triumphant main masquers, is a staged aristocratic dream vision rather than any recognizable depiction of native American life.[1]

The action of Chapman's masque unfolds between a stage set representing a New World island controlled by Indians of the Virginian "continent," an island from which the Indians come, and the British seat of state of King James at the hall's rear-center, the place to which the Indians triumphantly proceed. The featured performers, however, are neither the innocent, noble savages nor the monstrous primitives who, according to much political criticism, served as types of the strange "Other" and so prompted European acts of colonial control and repression. As New World rulers and worshippers of the sun, they are courtly aristocratic types who are identified as "Princes" and "Knights" and who perform as the social equals of the British aristocratic audience. The main masquers' courtly "habits," made from "cloath of siluer, richly embroidered, with golden Sunns," show only a touch of court-style "native" decoration in that there "ran a traile of gold, imitating Indian worke" about "euery Sunne"—an appropriate design gesture in otherwise traditional sumptuous masquing costumes (A2 verso). And they act as independent noble characters in a masquing world that, while abundant in natural wealth depicted in the main masque stage set, is conspicuously free of the colonial tyranny, sexual subjugation, drunkenness, slavery, oppression, cruelty and ethnic conflict that are the hallmark subjects of much recent political-literary criticism.

Even the New World antic performers who enter in a brief opening antimasque, though bizarre types suggestive of courtly Neapolitan intrigue, lack the evil malignancy of antiestablishment figures such as the witches in *The Masque of Queenes*. These New World antic figures are outlandish baboons "attir'd like fantasticall Trauailers, in Neopolitane sutes, and great ruffes." When their single "Anticke, and delightful" and seemingly gratuitous dance is over, they simply return to "their Tree" at the side of the stage (A).

The main masque that follows places the New World Virginian Indians "close to nature" in an unexpected way—a way doubtless longed for by James and members of his court, though certainly not anticipated by modern historians of the actual Virginia plantation. In an elaborate main masque stage spectacle, a rock transforms into a cloud. The cloud then "opens"; and to swelling music played by court musicians dressed as Priests of the Sun, the stately Indians are "discovered" within a radiant gold mine that glitters beneath a low, red sun.

Action is now "hinged," in the words of the masquing figure Honor, on the Virginian "Princes" coming to "Britan" to do "due homage" to the "*Lawe* and Vertue, celebrated" in the "sacred Nuptials" of the Princess Elizabeth and Frederick, and to pay homage in particular to the king who presides over both the marriage and the masque (D. 2). The work thus proceeds with the pacing of the masquers across the stage, their descent to the central hall for their main dances, and their triumphant presentation to and unmasking before the king.

The character Honor also debates with other figures over whether the hovering stage sun is rising or setting. The character "Eunomia," the "presenter" of the masquers and the personification of Law, prescriptively states the masque's thematic resolution, with which the featured performers through their symbolic movements show themselves in accord. In a speech using conventional masque sun iconography, Eunomia suggests that the stage sun will be seen rising when the ruling Virginian princes turn from past superstitions and, in a masquing triumph that implies a new political and religious allegiance, give their devotion to the personified true British sun which is "Enlightened with a Christian Piety."

> Virginian Princes, ye must now renounce
> Your superstitious worship of these Sunnes,
> Subject to cloudy darknings and descents,
> And of your sweet deuotions, turne the euents
> To this our Britain Phoebus (E)

Much could be said theoretically of Honor's admonition about what the Indians "must renounce" and to what they must "turn." It could be asserted, following the example of some recent critical approaches to *The Tempest* that "explain away" the work's internal contexts in order to give weight to external materials, that the masque's subterranean but now uncovered meaning and subtexts provide a central ideological statement on the power and politics of European colonialism. The masque would then point, in the light of wider historical "intertextualities," to the European subjugation of native Americans, destruction of the natives' religion and culture, and appropriation and exploitation of the natives' wealth and natural resources. And the masque could be seen to deny the very cultural existence of native Americans by making them nearly identical to Europeans.

But such claims, however meaningful as wide and general moral and political observations, would in turn unduly "suppress" the work's full contexts and its idealized main masque representation. In the golden world of Chapman's work, the island of the masque is *not* colonized. It is under the control of the aristocratic Indians, with personified gods and allegorical figures present but without the presence of colonizers. The Indians, in the manner of aristocratic performers in masque after masque, willingly and in festive triumph give their devotion of their own free will to the "state" identified with the sun. Their transfer of the object of their devotion from a lesser sun to a more glorious "Phoebus," another iconographic convention of main masques, is a festive act of free will. And after their choreographic compliment to the state—represented as a classical "Phoebus" Apollo imbued with inner "Christian Piety"—the masquers—Virginian Princes and Knights—can be assumed, as an inferred element of the masque fiction, to continue exercising local authority over their uncolonized homeland, but now under the aegis of the British sun king. Just how much the sun king would extract from their gold mine is open to question; here the masque indeed hints, by its graphic association of the Indians with gold, at the sun king's hopes of possibly obtaining native wealth. Finally, the typal "disguisings" of the main masque figures—Honor, Eunomia, the Indians, and the King as Phoebus—are all conventional generic fictions rather than realistic indexes to actual personal and social identities; and the Indians might well be regarded as receiving a compliment (rather than a dismissal) in being depicted as foreign, native aristocrats.

If the masque's dreamlike utopian political arrangements *were* compared to some form of actual government, then these arrangements might be seen as more reminiscent of an international commonwealth, in which native "Virginians" freely choose to recognize a foreign king while retaining local political authority, than of a colony in which natives are ruled by foreign occupying officials subject to a foreign monarch.

Considered as a masque written to flatter the king and court, the work is an imaginatively flamboyant and at times amusing construct of the new "open" court symbolism. Its romance elements are so phantasmagorical—mixing baboons dressed with ruffs, a gold mine, aristocratic Indians, and the king as the classical god Apollo—as to be surrealistic. Yet in directing attention to a New World so exotic it is historically unrecognizable, this late masque, mounted in the same year as *The Tempest*, might have caused persons familiar with that world and with voyage and colonial issues—possibly Shakespeare among them—to reflect upon actual New World problems involving the treatment of natives, the imposition of political power, and the expropriation of New World gold and natural resources. But it is also likely that at Whitehall in 1613, the masque would generally have been received as a stylized, celebratory, and ideologically conventional representation of how even aristocratic foreigners are drawn by honor and virtue to pay homage to and make bounty available to the glorious English king. What Chapman's masque most lucidly captures is a very special generic quality in main masque spectacles to which Shakespeare responded: an unrestrained and illusionary aristocratic utopianism that clearly called out for some kind of realistic modulation.

In *The Tempest,* Prospero seeks to control an imperfect world through his magic. Although critics, impressed and somewhat misdirected by Prospero's rhetoric, regularly lapse into the assumption that the Magus actually gives up the exercise of his powers at the beginning of the final scene, Prospero in fact has it both ways. He theatrically states in the present tense that he "abjures" his magic. But with his powers at their apex, he continues to use them, manipulating both events and characters to the very end of the dramatic action. He then promises, at the conclusion of scene 9, to employ his magic in the future to ensure clear sailing weather, though in the Epilogue immediately following he declares, in seeking the empathy of the audience, that his spells are "*ore-throwne*" (D. 19).

Before the final reconciliations that constitute a metaphoric rebirth, characters in the imperfect world of the play indulge themselves with social "imaginings." The essentially good counselor Gonzalo fancies an "antic" commonwealth of political and personal lassitude fortuitously supplied by a superabundant Nature. "I would with such perfection gouerne Sir," he remarks to Antonio, "T'Excell the Golden Age" (D. 7). Gonzalo's idle-man's commonwealth grows out of a cultural milieu of utopian works including Thomas More's communal *Utopia,* Robert Burton's agricultural commonwealth in the "Democritus" section of *The Anatomy of Melancholy,* tall tales of voyage authors about noble "primitive" societies; and polemical religious tracts predicting a coming millennium.[2] Gonzalo's reverie can also be seen more directly as a court counselor's satiric comment on the supposedly "perfect" hierarchical society revealed at the climax of familiar court theatricals such as Daniel's *The Vision of the 12. Goddesses* and Jonson's *Hymenaei* and *The Haddington Masque,* and in particular Jonson's later masque *The Golden Age Restored."*[3]

Stimulated by the word play of Antonio, Sebastian and Alonso, by talk of the lushness of the grass, and by the magical freshness of recently drenched garments, Gonzalo's casual social reveries on inaction and superabundance are rendered, as were court spectacles, "to minister occasion to these Gentlemen." His remarks are sharply antic. With his imagination amusingly active but his intellect seemingly at rest, Gonzalo announces that in his commonwealth he will "(by contraries)/Execute all things" (D. 7). The counselor would have "all men idle, all:/And Women too" (D. 7):

> All things in common Nature should produce
> Without sweat or endeuour: Treason, fellony,
> Sword, Pike, Knife, Gun, or neede of any Engine,
> Would I not haue: but Nature should bring forth
> Of it owne kinde, all foyzon, all abundance
> To feed my innocent people.
>
> (D. 7)

Despite Gonzalo's fanciful insistence that Nature should supply all in his imagined commonwealth, his past actions rationally contradict his fancy. Prospero has said earlier that Gonzalo humanely placed food in the small boat in which the Magus and Miranda had been set dangerously adrift by their enemies. The counselor took action to preserve their lives precisely because Nature could not be depended upon to do so.

Gonzalo's society of idleness, supposedly excelling the Golden Age, is eventually disclosed as a construction of negatives on an empty dream of "nothingness," a dream produced for the occasion with amusing but stinging overtones:

> . . . no kinde of Trafficke
> Would I admit: No name of Magistrate:
> Letters should not be knowne: Riches, poverty,
> And use of seruice, none; Contract, Succession,
> Borne, bound of Land, Tilth, Vineyard, none:
> No use of Mettall, Corne, or Wine, or Oyle:
> No occupation . . .
>
> (D. 7)

When Antonio mocks the counselor saying that he "dost talke nothing" (D. 7), Gonzalo in turn mocks the "sensible and nimble Lungs" of the gentlemen who "laugh at nothing" (D. 7). "'Twas you we laugh'd at," Antonio replies (D. 7). Gonzalo then strikes back, emphasizing the "nothingness" of the gentlemen's concerns, and implying that the men are fools associated with the moon, the source of madness.

Gonzalo's comments, with their ironic edge and their implication of egalitarian "leveling," are an original and mocking contrary to traditional iconography exalting an industrious, cultured and structured aristocratic-royalist state. But the "nothingness" of the words confirms that neither the imagined commonwealth nor its ideal contrary reflect actual social existence. The counselor's remarks thus satirically criticize even as they wittily entertain. They also hint at Gonzalo's inclination toward moral weakness: an excessive passivity in speaking against yet accepting corrupt nobles as masters. Here, central motifs—the emptiness of certain reveries, and the lunacy of those attending to them—foreshadow allusions to the emptiness of Caliban's vision and the comparative fullness of Prospero's.

In vivid contrast to Gonzalo's program for the mutual sharing of Nature's bounty, Caliban and his companions Trinculo and Stephano, ignoring others, basely and selfishly dream of hoarding the bounty of nature and mankind for themselves. Caliban gives vent to his earthly desires by paradoxically speaking of heavenly dreams. During a drunken conversation with Trinculo and Stephano, Caliban awkwardly describes the imagined descent of antic fools and virtuous figures from the changeable realm of the moon, the lowest and most material body in the Ptolemaic cosmos. Caliban's moon references thematically derive in part from traditional, exotic moon allusions in masques such as Jonson's *Masque of Blackness* (1605) and Thomas Campion's *Lord Hayes Masque*; and they anticipate those in Jonson's *News from the New World Discovered in the Moon* (1620).[4] In this last work, virtuous main masque moon people, the harbingers of an ideal Golden Age society, float down to earth and "shake off" their glittering silver "Isicles." Left behind on the moon, according to a Herald in the antimasque, are "two or three Moon-*Calves*!" (ll. 233–34). A character designated as Factor asks, "O, I, *Moone-Calves*! what Monster is that, I pray you?" To which the Herald replies, "Monster? none at all; a very familiar thing like our foole here on earth" (ll. 235–38).

In *The Tempest* Trinculo and Stephano, who are too gross even to "cut" the clouds in an abrupt descent, are imagined by an ignorant and foolish Caliban as gods who have directly descended by falling from above.

> Cal.: Ha'st thou not dropt from heauen?
>
> Ste. Out o'th Moon, I doe assure thee. I was the Man ith' Moone, when time was.
>
> Cal. I haue seene thee in her: and I doe adore thee. . . .
>
> (D. 10)

Caliban's foolish adoration of this spurious Man in the Moon is the antithesis of the monster's detestation of Prospero, who is seen as aided by the sun. Caliban curses the sun's brilliant light, and calls down upon Prospero those harmful "infections that the Sunne suckes vp" (D. 9). On the other hand, Caliban views Stephano as "a braue God" (D. 10), a figure who bears an all-too-earthly "liquor" that the monster in confusion says is "Celestiall." Caliban, in turn, is given an established "antic" lunar nickname by Stephano:

> How now, Moone-Calfe, how do's thine Ague?
>
> (D. 10)

Awkward, subhuman, earthly Caliban, adoring the base seamen and drinking their liquor, crassly imagines a Golden World of physical possessions and wealth—an island that he will own. And following the creature's reminiscence on the gradual "opening" of the heavens to instrumental music and voices as in a staged masque spectacle, he dreams of clouds dividing to reveal the mundane object of his desires:

> Cal. Be not affeard, the Isle is full of noyses,
> Sounds, and sweet aires, that giue delight and hurt not:
> Sometimes a thousand twangling Instruments
> Will hum about mine eares; and sometime voices,
> That if I then had wak'd after long sleepe,
> Will make me sleepe againe, and then, in dreaming,
> The clouds methought would open, and shew riches
> Ready to drop vpon me, that, when I wak'd,
> I cri'd to dreame again.
>
> (D. 12)

A comparable yet thematically different depiction of the masque-like opening of the heavens before shepherds occurs in Milton's *On the Morning of Christ's Nativity*. There, the "music sweet" of "Divinely warbled voice/Answering the stringed noise" is said by the poetic narrator to help the "fancy" envisage an "Age of Gold,"[5] an age that in this case is represented as spiritually transcendent. The music in Milton's poem introduces the "discovery" of heavenly cherubim and seraphim within a "globe of circular light"; and this discovery is followed by the appearance in the scenic heavens of the theological figures Faith, Hope, and Mercy who then descend to earth on "tissued clouds down steering" (ll. 146–47).

Although critics seeking to show empathetic qualities in Caliban rightly suggest that the monster reacts with humane delight to "sounds and sweet airs," they overlook the fact that Caliban's allusions to instrumental and vocal music are but the matrix for the culminating masque-like depiction of the monster's flawed ideal. The noisy "twangling" and the "hum" of stringed instuments, followed by the sound of voices, stir in Caliban dreams of clouds opening, not upon virtuous figures ready gracefully to descend to an honored viewer, but rather upon material riches ready to "drop" on a dreamer. And, too, they overlook a remark by Stephano on the music in Caliban's fanciful "brave kingdom," that echoes again the theme of "nothingness."

Ste. This will proue a braue kingdome to me,
Where I shall haue my Musicke for nothing.

(D. 12)

In the later betrothal masque—the antitype of Caliban's antic dream and Gonzalo's antic reveries—Prospero's representation of a Golden Age marriage can be seen in tune with a virtuous conception of nature and society.

Before the masque begins, Prospero warns Ferdinand to beware of brutish lust engendered by "th' fire ith' blood" (D. 14). Ferdinand states and subsequently demonstrates that he can indeed suppress burning passion by restraining "the ardour of my Liuer" (D. 14), one of the supposed "seats" of fiery desire. However, passion and lust have flamed in other characters earlier. In scene 2, Prospero wrathfully condemns the monster for attempting to rape Miranda. Later, Caliban, Trinculo and Stephano plot sedition and murder after becoming, in the words of Ariel, "red-hot with drinking" (D. 15).

By contrast, the betrothal masque features iconography suggestive of a cool, restrained, chaste love appropriate to the honored couple, and antithetical to the fiery passions that in earlier scenes spurred Caliban's lust and desire for riches and power. An aristocratic vision of peace, harmony and plenitude centered on a new theme—the bearing of children—now briefly supplants and suppresses Prospero's awareness of the reality of Caliban's sedition and obsessions. In the masque it is the mother goddess Juno who, in gracefully descending and then in blessing the betrothed couple, gives rich expression to ideals of honor, prosperity, joy and, most important, human and earthly plenitude.

Iu. Honor, riches, marriage, blessing,
Long continuance, and encreasing,
Hourly yes, be still upon you,
Juno sings her blessings on you
Earth's increase, poison plenty
Barrens, and Garners, near empty.
Vines, with clustering bunches growing,

> *Plants, with goodly berthed bowing:*
> *Spring come to you at the farthest,*
> *In the very end of Hairiest.*
> *Scarcity and want shall shun you,*
> Ceres *blessing so is on you.*
>
> (D. 15)

In *Anthony and Cleopatra*, the passionate and moody Cleopatra, at the moment of her death, identifies with the element that was thought to burn with varying intensity in human beings. "I am Fire and Ayre," she declares, "my other Elements/I giue to baser life" (D. 367). Throughout *The Tempest*, it is precisely the element of fire, with its power to cause the heat of burning desire, that Prospero seeks to keep at a distance from cool and chaste Miranda. In conjuring up the masque, the Magus thus banishes from the stage—while allowing their names to be mentioned—two other characters associated with fiery passion: "*Marses* hot Minion" (D. 14), that is, the goddess Venus; and her son Cupid. Prospero features Iris, Ceres and Juno as main masquers, each of them associated with an element other than fire. Iris with her "refreshing showers" and "watry Arch" carries iconographic allusions to water; Ceres, with her "Medes" "bankes" and "Turfie-Mountaines," the earth; and Juno, the "Queene o'th Skie" who descends, the air (D. 14).

Although Iris and Ceres are distinctive in the betrothal masque in speaking slightingly of Venus and Cupid, they are otherwise presented as traditional iconographic figures of, respectively, the rainbow and earthly fertility, in consonance with their established roles in works as varied as Virgil's *Aeneid*, Ovid's *Metamorphosis*, and in Daniel's *The Vision of the 12. Goddesses* and *Tethys Festival*, and Ben Jonson's *Hymenaei*. Shakespeare's Juno appears most indebted to Jonson. In the text of Daniel's *Vision of the 12. Goddesses*, Juno was represented primarily as a figure of divine power without specific attributes, but in Jonson's marriage masque *Hymenaei*, the goddess directly signifies those meanings prominent in *The Tempest*: "ayre" and, through an anagram, "union." In the words of the figure Reason in Jonson's masque,

> And see where IVNO, whose great name
> Is VNIO, in the *anagram*,
> Displayes her glistering state, and chaire,
> As she enlightened all the ayre!
>
> (ll. 232–35)

Jonson may well have induced Shakespeare to develop long-recognized anagrams of his own. It seems likely that Shakespeare introduced the name Caliban as an anagram for "Canibal," in the seventeenth century usage of the word, a "sauage" (D. 5) living close to the earth. The contrasting name Prospero appears to be an anagram for "Prosperity." It is the name "*Prosper*" that Alonso thinks he hears echoing within the sound of thunder when Ariel, disguised as a harpy, vanishes in scene 7 (D. 13). In the next scene, when the betrothal masque is interrupted by Prospero's thought of the seditious Caliban, thematic oppositions in the play are further underlined by the roles and names of these two figures.

The idealized but interrupted betrothal masque briefly but memorably highlights Prospero's unattainable, evanescent dream of social harmony. Shakespeare, here and earlier, artfully chooses and intermingles masque-like hieroglyphics to insure social meanings adjusted to his own theatrical purposes.

Prospero's movement from fury to reconciliation in the play's last scene is not powerful drama. A passing comment by Ariel about the sadness of the wandering nobles spurs the Magus to follow his human feelings.

> Ar. . . . your charm so strongly works 'em
> That if you now beheld them, your affections
> Would become tender
>
> (D. 16)

The Magus's reply is surprisingly casual: "Dost thou thinke so Spirit?" To which Ariel says, "Mine would, Sir, were I humane" (D. 16). Prospero suddenly declares, "And mine shall." Yet before rationally deciding on the "sole drift" of his "purpose," the Magus, as if out of a need to convince himself of his own "affections," asks a self-reflective rhetorical question:

> Hast thou (which art but aire) a touch, a feeling
> Of their afflictions, and shall not my selfe,
> One of their kinde, that relish all as sharpely,
> Passion as they, be kindlier mou'd then thou art?
>
> (D. 16)

The question proves decisive. Prospero avows in only five lines that he is "strook to th' quick" by fury but will now take action relying upon his "nobler reason" (D. 16). The change is introduced, not as a deeply felt dramatized experience, but as a quick and rather matter-of-fact reasoned decision that leads into a series of dominating, ritualistic, magical actions.

On the private stage at Blackfriars or the public stage at the Globe, actors with only these few lines to work with might imaginatively improvise and act out an emotional change that is only haltingly suggested by Prospero's brief, flat questions and remarks. But at Whitehall on the uplifted royal stage, and particularly on the green rug of the center-hall performing space, performers in close proximity to the audience could have emphasized the change memorably through the magical rituals, "presentations" and "unmaskings" that were a climactic part of Whitehall Spectacle Triumphs.

In the opening lines of the play's final scene, the Magus, in full magical regalia, proclaims that his zenith of power has at last arrived. He now turns to the magical resolution of his "Proiect" at the evensong hour of Vespers as day fades into night.

> Now do's my Proiect gather to a head:
> My charms cracke not; my Spirits obey, and Time
> Goes vpright with his carriage: how's the day?

> Ar. On the sixt hower; at which time, my Lord,
> You said our worke should cease.
>
> (D. 16)

This resolution begins with rituals of "robing" and empowerment. Ariel had earlier been ordered to Prospero's Cell to obtain the magical robes that Prospero called "trumpery" and that Trinculo subsequently called "wardrobe" (D. 15), a term often used for theatrical costumes. The garments were donned by the comic conspirators in an antic mockery of true kingship. But now in this final scene of the play, the robes are most seriously assumed by Prospero in his role as Magus as he apparently displays his instruments of power: a magical wand and an occultist book.

Even Caliban had recognized the force of Prospero's magic; the monster had insisted that the overthrow of the Magus depended upon the destruction of his occult books. "Braine him," the monster declared, "Having first seiz'd his bookes." Caliban twice repeated this admonition. "Remember/First to possesse his Bookes; for without them/ He's but a Sot"; "Burne but his Bookes" (D. 12).

In the final scene, after having donned his magical robes, Prospero, stepping forward from his Cell, makes his great declamation on the terrible strength of his occult power. Echoing the "Chief Dame's" magical claims in the *Masque of Queenes* (ll. 218–43) and the sorceress Medea's praise of magical art in the *Metamorphosis* (7.197–219), Prospero announces that his "rough Magicke" has "bedymm'd" the sun, called forth "windes" that stired the seas, and even raised the shades of the dead.

> . . . Graues at my command
> Haue wak'd their sleepers, op'd, and let 'em forth
> By my so potent Art.
>
> (D. 16)

For many in court and public audiences and very possibly for James I himself, Prospero's necromantic recalling the dead to life would have been viewed as blasphemously mirroring Christ's raising of Lazarus as recorded in Scripture. Earlier in the scene, Prospero had been addressed by Ariel as "my Lord," the title applied to Christ in Patristic commentary.

> . . . how's the day?
>
> Ar. On the sixt hower; at which time, my Lord,
> You said our worke should cease.
>
> (D. 16)

According to all four Gospel accounts, it was at the sixth hour that, as Christ hung crucified on the Cross, darkness came over the earth and the graves gave up their dead. In the words of the Gospel of Matthew, which are echoed in the Gospels of Mark and Luke,

> Now from the sixth hour there was darkness over all the land unto the ninth hour. (27.45)
>
> And the graves were opened; and many bodies of the saints which slept arose. (27.52)[6]

Yet Prospero's actions are the reverse of those of the crucified Christ of Scripture—and the reverse of those of the changeable figure Medea in Ovid's Latin poem the *Metamorphosis*. In the Bible, Christ's Passion ultimately results in a disclosure of divinity that overcomes death and reveals an eternal kingdom. In Ovid's poem, Medea exercises her demonic magical powers to restore the youth of aging Aeson, the father of her husband Jason. Overtones of these scriptural and poetic allusions resonate in the play. But in actions that are the antithesis of Christ's scriptural victory over death and revelation of a heavenly kingdom, and of Medea's restoration of Aeson's youth in Ovid's work, Prospero, like a main masquer removing a visor and disclosing a human face, strips away his screening weeds as Magus, "abjures" and so renounces occult necromantic and other magical powers, and comes forward in his social role as Duke of Milan and as a frail and aging human being. Prospero ultimately acts out of virtue rather than fury, but there remains about the Magus and his magic a moral ambivalence. Prospero has performed virtuous works of reconciliation while admitting to the raising of tempests and the dead. These last actions would have been recognized as blasphemous deeds of black and necromantic magic in violation of God's natural law, deeds that certainly would have been condemned by King James and officials of his court.[7]

And Prospero, having verbally "abjured" his rough magic, continues to promote virtuous results through dubious occult means. When Prospero confronts his enemies, the confused nobles are reconciled to the Magus not through dramatic acted-out demonstrations of anguish or love, but rather through the jolting experience of Prospero's magic. The Magus confirms that Alonso is still under a spell and so subject to the "subtilties" or illusions of the island. In this state Alonso asks "pardon" for his "wrongs" and thereupon directly resigns the falsely gained Dukedom of Milan in favor of the rightful Duke Prospero. But in telling his "strange story," Alonso confesses that the affliction of his mind and his past madness have been overcome by the astonishing magical reappearance of Prospero, referred to here as an apparent phantom or "inchanted trifle" (D. 17). When Alonso asks for forgiveness, the Magus actually intervenes to prevent him from delving introspectively into memories of past evil.

> Alo. I
> Must aske my child forgiuenesse;
>
> Pro. There, Sir, stop,
> Let vs not burthen our remembrances, with
> A heauiness that's gon.
>
> (D. 18)

A sense of the miraculous pervades the scene. Prospero's magic so awes the nobles that, in the words of the Magus, "they deuoure their reason and scarse thinke." And Prospero, in a comment recalling the paramount role Inigo Jones gave to the "eyes" in achieving spiritual enlightenment, repeats a truism of court iconographic stagecraft:

"Their eies doe offices of Truth" (D. 17). The enchanter then inspires amazement by producing "a wonder": magically presenting Miranda and Ferdinand playing chess. "A most high miracle," Sebastian cries upon seeing the seemingly drowned Ferdinand resurrected and in the company of this unknown young maid (D. 17).

This unexpected "wonder" appealing for its "Truth" to the eyes rather than the other senses would very likely have been mounted at Whitehall at a central rear-stage position as a sudden "discovery." If traditional staging techniques were followed at court, backflats or perhaps a curtain would have been quickly drawn to disclose the betrothed couple in an iconographic tableau. Lambent light cast by oil lamps or candles may well have illumined Ferdinand and Miranda, now perhaps dressed in conventional sparkling outer garments covered with reflecting metal "orbs" or "spangs," as they revealed their inner virtue through gracious movements even while playing at the battle game of chess. Some years later in Thomas Middleton's allegorical *A Game of Chess* (1624), a play satirizing the machinations of the English and Spanish courts' marriage negotiations, performers acted out the roles of belligerent chess pieces. At Whitehall, the iconographic "speaking picture" would have signified the spiritual chastity of Miranda in her reactions to the seemingly playful deceptions of her betrothed at the gaming board.

> Mir. Sweet Lord, you play me false.
>
> Fer. No my dearst loue,
> I would not for the world.
>
> Mir. Yes, for a score of Kingdomes, you should wrangle,
> And I would call it faire play.
>
> (D. 17)

Together, the iconography and dialogue demonstrate that in earthly play at chess, even as in earthly love, there resides the potential for mortal corruption.

Not long afterward, Miranda, looking upon mortals other

than her father for the first time, experiences astonishment. "O wonder!" she exclaims (D. 17). Alonso, stunned by the visionary appearance of his son Ferdinand whom he thought drowned, desires deep oracular understanding of the events. But again Prospero prevents immediate introspective knowledge, directing Alonso's sensibility away from intellectual comprehension and toward magical experience.

> Alo. . . . there is in this busnesse, more than nature
> Was euer conduct of: some Oracle
> Must rectifie our knowledge.
>
> Pro. Sir, my Liege,
> Doe not infest your minde, with beating on
> The strangenesse of this businesse; at pickt leisure
> (Which shall be shortly single) I'le resolue you,
> (Which to you shall seeme probable) of euery
> These happend accidents: till when, be cheerful
> And thinke each thing well
>
> (D. 18)

Even the last entrance of Caliban inspires amazement. "This is a strange thing," Alonso remarks, "as eer I look'd on" (D. 18).

In *The Winter's Tale*, King Leontes of Sicilia, by seeking and receiving a message from the Delphic Oracle, obtains deep prophetic knowledge of his own misdeeds. But in *The Tempest* such deep knowledge is deferred. Rather, the immediate experience of wondrous events followed by the gradual emergence of amazed characters from spells and illusions to a recognition of true identities, provides a gradual dawning, but not a full illumination, of intellectual insight. Shakespeare, playing upon spectacle traditions of magical transformation, uses the "unmasking" of identities as a metaphor for spiritual rebirth. He thus gives to his drama the general theme of human regeneration familiar to ancient mystery plays, but not by making explicit allusions to such dramas. He relies instead upon immediately known masque forms, devices and ceremonial actions.

In this way, Alonso slowly begins to recognize the true

identities of Miranda and Prospero as they symbolically "unmask." Having witnessed the astonishing "discovery" of Miranda playing at chess, Alonso is puzzled. "What is this Maid," he asks his son, "with whom thou was't at play?"

> Is she the goddesse that hath seuer'd vs,
> And brought vs thus together?
>
> (D. 18)

Miranda's magical "discovery" has indeed been like that of a virtuous goddess in a masque, one whose absence has allowed for past antic action, but one whose surprise entry and power restore social harmony. Ferdinand, speaking as someone spiritually reborn through his "second father" Prospero, now strips the screening disguise from Miranda and presents her in her underlying human reality:

> Sir, she is mortall;
> But by immortall prouidence, she's mine:
> I chose her when I could not aske my Father
> For his aduice, nor thought I had one: She
> Is daughter to this famous Duke of Millaine,
> Of whom, so often I have heard renowne,
> But neuer saw before: of whom I haue
> Receiu'd a second life; and second Father
>
> (D. 18)

Gonzalo joins in underscoring the play's theme of discovery and unmasking by adding that "In one voyage" many persons and things were found, among them, "all of vs our selues/When no man was his owne" (D. 18). With the final visionary entrance of Miranda at the end of the nobles' wanderings, "all" of the aristocrats are symbolically "unmasked" to themselves and restored to their own identities. The confused seamen who also now appear, having been aroused by Ariel from enchanted sleep, experience a wondrous reawakening to themselves and to all around them. And when a distracted Caliban wearing the Magus's stolen clothing is driven on stage together with Stephano and Trinculo, the monster is at first verbally chastised by Prospero. But then, as the Magus again assumes the role of a "second Father," Caliban is greeted by Prospero as "mine" and promised pardon. Caliban, seeing the figure he now calls his "fine . . . Master" transformed in appearance by state robes, is himself astonishingly transformed. Caliban alone among the play's characters announces, with possible religious undertones, that he will "be wise hereafter,/ And seeke for grace" (D. 18–19).

An air of uncertainty nonetheless remains, for much has been left unexplained. Prospero has promised Alonso growing revelations in times to come; in addition, the Magus promises ever-expanding knowledge from his personal tale.

> Alo. I long
> To hear the story of your life; which must
> Take the eare strangely.
>
> Pro. I'le deliuer all.
>
> (D. 19)

Prospero's wondrous magic will continue too, for the Magus announces that he will engage in one more extraordinary exercise of his art before he breaks his staff and drowns his book. He will, with the help of Ariel, give Alonso

> calm Seas, auspicious gales
> And saile so expeditious, that shall catch
> Your Royall fleete farre off. My *Ariel*, chicke,
> That is thy charge; Then to the Elements
> Be free, and fare thou well:
>
> (D. 19)

In the magical calm that follows the tempest, charmed winds will waft Prospero and the reconciled nobles from the Mediterranean island of utopian dreams. Ariel will be free to return to the elements; and Caliban, to occupy the island that the creature coveted. The strange, revealing tale that Prospero promises to tell, as he breaks from the realm of illusion to reenter the mainland world, is left mysteriously unspoken at the end of the play.

The play's Epilogue, even more than the "entries" and "unmaskings" of characters in the drama's last scene, shows the tensions Shakespeare faced in adapting the social forms of the masquing Triumph to a staged drama. The Triumph forms produced a pressure to create plays in which there was an actual break from the theatrical world of romance and dream into the actual social world of the audience in the hall. In turn, the counterpressures of dramatic form required a certain aesthetic distance between audience and performers, even in the Epilogue.

Shakespeare responded by composing a play in which the "release" of performers into the actual society of spectators in the hall is never complete. There are no revels in which the commoners who were actors totally unmask—that is, fully cast off the screen of their make-believe identities and enter into the court as known persons in an existing social hierarchy. The actors remain theatrical character-types whose entry into the social world essentially takes place in the context of the drama. It is Prospero alone who, having disclosed himself as the "true" Duke of Milan, unmasks sufficiently to reveal, beneath the theatrical guise of the Duke, an elder actor pointedly appealing to an audience for applause and prayers. In the Epilogue, when Prospero briefly reappears alone to ask that the "good hands" of the audience release him from the magical "bands" still confining him, his request is more than an emotive appeal for applause (D. 19). It is an appeal for permission to break further from the constraining illusions of the play. And at Whitehall, the actor would very likely have made this personal plea, not from a raised stage as is often assumed, but close to the audience from the central green rug bordering the tiers or degrees on which the aristocrats were seated. The performer then would have been in a position to make a final step that was in fact barred to him as an actor and a commoner—the troubling step at the root of tensions in applying the masque to dramatic form—the step over the carpet's edge and into an actual aristocratic society.

Such tensions are echoed in the social world within the play. The innocent Miranda may believe in seeming harbingers of a "braue new world" into which she is about to enter; but Prospero dryly remarks, "'Tis new to thee" (D. 17–18). And in the Epilogue, when the Magus asks for the prayers of the audience, he is sadly considering the possibility of his own future despair. For in *The Tempest*, the social realm now contained within the play allows for the continuing existence of ideals of innocence and virtuous union; but it is a social realm with a potential for war and sedition mirroring that of the external world, and it is a social realm in which divine providence is invoked by Prospero in recognition of human mortality.

EPILOGUE

In "A short discourse on the English Stage" published in 1664, Richard Flecknoe, the poet and playwright so notoriously mocked in John Dryden's poem *MacFlecknoe*, harshly disparaged certain developments in the British stage by comparing the "plain" pre-Commonwealth theaters of Shakespeare's period to the supposedly magnificent theaters of his own time. Outward scenic splendor and ornament, Flecknoe complained, had replaced dramatic substance.

> Now, for the difference betwixt our Theaters and those of former times, they were but plain and simple, with no other Scenes, not Decorations of the Stage, but onely old Tapestry, and the Stage strew'd with Rushes, (with their Habits accordingly) whereas ours now for cost and ornament are arriv'd to the height of Magnificence; but that which makes our Stage the better, makes our Playes the worse perhaps, they striving now to make them more for sight thn hearing; whence that solid joy of the interior is lost, and that benefit which men formerly receiv'd from Playes, from which they seldom or never went away, but far better and wiser thn they came.[1]

Although Flecknoe's rigid moralism and insensitivity to highly stylized drama left him open to the very charge of shallowness he leveled against others, he was no doubt correct in asserting that the English theater had begun to concentrate on the visual. Beginning generally in the 1660s and extending into the eighteenth century, the indoor, decorated, framed stages of the public and private theaters enclosed pictorial moveable scenery, featured fire and water effects and levitation devices, and were well-stocked with traps and stage properties. Women as well as men appeared on the illuminated apron stages, which fronted audiences seated in rows, to sing or recite musical numbers that often imaginatively invoked exotic locales and characters.

The extraordinary career of William Davenant, who adapted *The Tempest* for this kind of stage, in itself provides an overview of the sweeping theatrical transitions that occurred in the space of some 40 years. Davenant, a royalist, displayed unusual ingenuity in devising different types of new stage works and remained theatrically active through the monarchy and Commonwealth and into the Restoration.

In 1630, just 17 years after the original *Tempest* was performed for the marriage of Princess Elizabeth, this playwright-poet penned two relatively conventional dramas, *The cruell brother* and *The ivst Italian*, obviously designed for bare-stage production with a minimum of properties. While continuing to write plays of this sort, he also in 1635 replaced Ben Jonson as a writer of court masques, composing five masques in five years. The last was the extravagantly staged *Salmacida Spoila* (1640), the final masquing triumph mounted at court at great expense before the revolution. During the Commonwealth era, Davenant invented novel theatrical works to circumvent the ban on staged dramas. Labeling his initial creation—clearly a mixed theatrical form —an "opera," and so gaining approval for private London presentation, he added music and song to declamatory speeches and in May 1656, produced *The First Day's entertainment at Rutland House.* This was quickly followed in August of the same year by a more finished "opera," the first part of *The Siege of Rhodes*, presented again at Rutland House against drawn stage scenic flats with

Mrs. Coleman singing the role of Ianthe. Music, moveable stage sets and rich properties now became a regular feature of Davenant's works as, for example, in the curious historical "opera" *The history of Sr Francis Drake Exprest by instrumentall and vocall musick and by art of perspective in scenes* (1659).

After the theatre companies were allowed to resume performing dramas in 1660, Davenant, obtaining a patent to establish the Duke of York's players, collaborated with John Dryden to write and elaborately stage a new version of *The Tempest, or the Enchanted Island.* With controls over the theatres loosened, the collaborators in November 1667 were able to present this "heroic drama"—reduced in suggestiveness and adapted to audience desires for stylization and spectacle, at the well-equipped Duke of York's Theatre complete with dances, songs and full-stage scenic effects depicting a tempest at sea, a ship sinking, a shower of fire, a sun rising and figures flying simultaneously in the air.[2] In the light of such theatrical developments, Shakespeare's *The Tempest* remained a pivotal play, its allusions and stage directions anticipating audience interests in song, dance, magic, spectacle and strange and exotic themes—interests politically repressed during the Commonwealth, but interests that increasingly gained in popular appeal and again broke forth with unusual force during the Restoration.

Like Davenant, Shakespeare responded to the multiple, shifting influences of court and theater in his day, but he responded in a more dramatically adroit manner, using the new open symbolism of the spectacles theatrically to project unsettling and seemingly inexplicable experiences of wonder and awe, to give external symbolic expression to the fancies and corrupt or ideal dreams of the characters, and finally to stress the inadequacy of all such fanciful utopian visions, when bereft of both prayer and grace, given the transience of human life.

The Tempest, with its spectacles of strangeness, is neither a definitive return by Shakespeare to the academic play of his early years nor an advanced dramatic adaptation or superimposition of the antimasque-main masque form of Jonson. Rather, Shakespeare, imaginatively aware of performance requirements of the public and private theatres but particularly of the court stage at Whitehall, adapted old pageant *intermezzo* elements to the drama, and so created a work of interspersed spectacles of strangeness and order, a play "hinged" upon magic, replete with ritualistic action, filled with individualized characters of typal origins, imaginatively reflective of court stage devices and scenic settings, and climaxed by the "revelation" and reconciliation of central characters in a new kind of dramatized Spectacle Triumph.

The Tempest thus comes down to readers as a brilliantly evocative transitional drama that, in its originality and symbolic richness, is ultimately subject to its own unique internal structures and meanings. In writing what was probably his final play, Shakespeare chose well.

Notes

Notes to Introduction

1. Rather than rely on edited versions of *The Tempest* compiled from a mixture of pages from different printed copies of the 1623 Folio, or from edited versions containing interposed stage directions and line references, I have taken all citations from the original leaf pages of *The Tempest* in *Mr. William Shakespeares Comedies, Histories, & Tragedies. Published according to the True Originall Copies*, the Chatsworth copy of the Duke of Devonshire, dedication and introduction by John Heminge and Henrie Condell (London: Issac Iaggard, and Ed. Blount, 1623), Huntington Library Collection 56399. "D." for Devonshire replaces "p." or "pp." in all references to pagination, with every reference to Jonson's poem "To the memory of . . ." from the Devonshire edition's unnumbered opening pages. Consulted also were the 1623 Halsey copy, Huntington 56420; the 1623 Bridgewater copy, Huntington 56421; and the 1623 Mary S. Harkness copy, New York Public Library.

In an introduction to the Chatsworth facsimile edition, *Shakespeares Comedies, Histories, & Tragedies* (Oxford, 1902), Sidney Lee concludes, after having conducted a census of extant Folio copies, that the Chatsworth copy is "probably the cleanest and freshest exemplar in existence. Every leaf is in the original state, but seven consecutive leaves in the section on tragedy were inserted from a second shorter copy to fill a gap, which accident at some early date caused in the volume after it came from the press" (xxxv). No citations in the present article are from the inserted pages.

Citations of Early Modern rare books like the Chatsworth 1623 Folio will include the printer.

The copy here employed was acquired by the Henry E. Huntington Library from the Duke of Devonshire's Library at Chatsworth in 1916. The copy had formerly belonged to the collector, the Duke of Roxburghe, who had purchased it in 1790 at auction from the library of John Watson Reed, an attorney in Ely Place, London. Its earlier provenance is unknown. See Sidney Lee's *A Census of Extant Copies: A Supplement to the Reproduction in Facsimile of the First Folio Edition (1623) from the Chatsworth Copy* . . . (London, 1902), 8–9, for an analysis of the known facts about the copy.

Very minute differences caused by the occasional correction of type as it was passing through the press—differences involving usually one letter in a word and very minor occasional changes in punctuation and marking—appear in many of the approximately 230 Folio copies surviving from an original seventeenth century printing of an estimated 1,200 copies. The differences in the printing of marks and words, as evident in the 80 Folio copies in the Folger Library examined by Charlton Hinman in *The Printing and Proof-Reading of the First Folio of Shakespeare*, 2 vols. (Oxford, 1963) and as evident too in the original copies consulted by this writer, are indeed slight and do not result in variations in the meaning or tonality of words or passages quoted in this book from the Chatsworth copy. Page numbers cited for just *The Tempest* are sometimes duplicated in the pagination of other plays in the Folio.

See the "mixed" edition of 1623 Folio prepared by Charlton Hinman in *The Norton Facsimile: The First Folio of Shakespeare* (New York, 1968) from what he believed to be the "best" 29 Folio copies, out of the 80 Folio copies in the Folger Library collection, but without employing the approximately 150 remaining extant copies. Each page in the Hinman edition is included as the most satisfactory example of that page, as determined by the editor, from among the 29 Folio copies actually used. See also Hinman, "Why 79 First Folios?," a mimeographed lecture in the collection of the Huntington Library (PR 2892.1 H5) that was originally given before the Bibliographical Society of the University of Virginia, 6 June 1947.

2. Munday, *The Triumphs of a Re-United Britain* (London: W. Jaggard, 1605), title page. See also the "Triumph" in John Nichols, *The Progresses, Processions, and Magnificent Festivities of King James the First*, vol. 1 (London: Printed for the Society of Antiquaries, 1628), 305.

3. Campion, "*The Description* of a Maske: Presented in the

Banqueting roome at *Whitehall* on Saint Stephens night last, at the mariage of the Right Honourable Earle of Somerset: And the right noble the Lady Frances Howard" (London: Printed by E. A. for *Lawrence Li'sle,* 1614), unnumbered page. Among the character-types in the masque, described on the same page as Europe, are figures representing the four elements of Earth, Air, Fire and Water.

4. E. K. Chambers, *William Shakespeare,* 2 vols. (Oxford, 1930) 2.342; for comments on the dating and performances of the play, see 1.491–92, and also Frank Kermode, ed., *The Tempest* (London, 1964), xxi–xxii.

5. Public Records Office (PRO), Audit Office, Declared Accounts, Bundle 389, Roll 49, fol. 10b.

6. See Chambers, *William Shakespeare,* 2.343.

7. In readings focused on Caliban in the light of European colonialism, the monster, seen as the one-time oppressor of Miranda in earlier traditional criticism, emerges as the oppressed victim. Leo Marx in "Shakespeare's American Fable," *The Machine in the Garden* (London: Oxford, 1964), 34–72; and Harry Levin in *The Myth of the Golden Age in the Renaissance* (Bloomington, 1967), 121–29, argue that the drama contains European stereotypes of New World inhabitants as either innocent or bestial, and that Prospero exhibits European attitudes in seeking to understand "uncivilized" human nature in terms of these types. Leslie A. Fiedler in *The Stranger in Shakespeare* (New York, 1972), 233–51, continues the discussion of typal representation, analyzing Caliban as the victimized and feared "Stranger" comparable to Shakespearean theatrical depictions of a number of Jews, Moors, and women who are also "outsiders."

In an interpretation that judges Caliban "externally" in terms of the monster's importance to colonial and historical discourse rather than "internally" and dramatically in terms of the monster's role in the play, Terence Hawkes in "Swisser-Swatter: making a man of I acknowledge mine'," *Alternative Shakespeares,* ed. John Drakakis (London, 1985), 191–205, sees Caliban as a pejorative type of the native, central in European colonial efforts to demonize, exploit and extract wealth from local inhabitants of the New World. This is further examined by Thomas Cartelli in "Prospero in Africa: *The Tempest* as Colonialist Text and Pretext" in *Shakespeare Reproduced: Europe and the native Caribbean: 1492–1797* (London and New York, 1986), 88–134; and by Paul Brown, "This Thing of Darkness I Acknowledge Mine: *The Tempest* and the Discourse of Colonialism," in *Political Shakespeare: Essays in Cultural Materialism,* ed. Jonathan Dollimore and Alan Sinfield, 2nd ed. (Manchester, 1994), 48–71.

For further references to Hawkes and to colonial readings, see chapter 2, n. 11.

8. See the text and notes of William M. Hamlin's "Men of Inde: Renaissance Ethnography and *The Tempest*," in *Shakespeare Studies*, ed. Leeds Barroll, vol. 22 (London and Toronto, 1984), in which the author maintains that Caliban only somewhat reflects presumed stereotypical bestial qualities in colonized natives and becomes increasingly human as the play progresses. Accepting some of the New World and colonial allusions or intimations in the play out of the many that have been critically proposed, Hamlin nevertheless takes exception to those core colonial interpretations that "tend to condemn too categorically other readings as ahistorical while remaining dogmatic in their own insistence." He accurately notes that in such "core" interpretations, "moral and sociopolitical agendas often predetermine their conclusions" (20).

Stephen Greenblatt writing as a New Historicist, and Meredith Anne Skura as a critic influenced by traditional commentary and also somewhat by Frederic Jameson's revisionist interpretations, have both respectively branded as "problematic" recent claims that *The Tempest* considered intertextually clearly mirrors actual colonized lands. Skura in "Discourse and the Individual," *Shakespeare Quarterly* 4, no. 1 (Spring, 1989): 42–69, observes that "recent criticism not only flattens the play into the mold of colonialist discourse and eliminates what is characteristically 'Shakespearean,' but it is also—paradoxically—in danger of taking the play further from the particular historical situation in England in 1611 even as it brings it closer to what we mean by 'colonialism' today" (47). She adds that her aim is "not to deny that the play has any relation" to "colonialist discourse" of the 1611 period, discourse which she finds "mediated" in the play by what she calls Shakespeare's "unique mind," but rather "to suggest that the relation is problematic" (57). Skura underscores her position by emphasizing that "we have no external evidence that seventeenth century audiences thought the play referred to the New World" (47).

In *Learning to Curse: Aspects of Linguistic Colonialism in the Sixteenth Century* (New York and London, 1990), Greenblatt notes that "many aspects of the play itself . . . make colonialism a problematical model for the theatrical imagination: if *The Tempest* holds up a mirror to empire, Shakespeare would appear deeply ambivalent about using the reflected image as a representation of his own practice" (24). Greenblatt accordingly turns his attention, not to any problematic "reflected image" of the New World in the play, but rather to rhetorical issues of what he calls "colonial linguistics."

See Skura on "familial colonialism," and Greenblatt on "colonial linguistics," in chapter 1, n. 11.

9. In a comprehensive analysis of the history of Shakespeare criticism on Caliban that includes a critique of the range of recent colonial interpretations, Alden T. Vaughan and Virginia Mason Vaughan in *Shakespeare's Caliban: A Cultural History* (Cambridge, 1991), particularly in the chapter "Colonial Metaphors" (144–71), find that "the principal dilemma that faced users of Tempest (and especially Caliban) metaphors in the third quarter of the twentieth century was postcolonial self-fashioning" (147). They note that commentators seek a universalism that can be applied to modern views on colonialism, a universalism usually not based on the full context of the play or on its documented contemporaneous historical background. They conclude that such criticism is "not historic" (146–47), and that Caliban does not "symbolize any particular person, group, or quality, but rather a general *unruliness* in society and nature" (278).

See also Brian Vickers's encompassing review and bibliography of recent colonialist and political readings of *The Tempest* in *Appropriating Shakespeare: Contemporary Critical Quarrels* (New Haven, 1993), especially 165–213, 242–48, and 415–16. Writing generally of what he calls the "combative nature" of the modern poststructuralist movement and, in his view, its attempted political appropriation of Shakespeare in support of contemporary causes, he maintains that "its real goal" was "to attack the systems of ideas which then held place, interpreted as instruments of power and repression, rather than develop a more sensitive or perceptive approach to literature" (xiii). See other comments criticizing the alleged modern political appropriation of Shakespeare in Diana Bryden, "Re-Writing *The Tempest*," *World Literature Written in England* no. 23 (1984): 75–88; Edward Pechter, "The New Historicism and its Discontents: Politicizing Renaissance Drama," *PMLA* 102 (1987): 292–303; and Jean Howard, "The New Historicism in Renaissance Studies," *English Literary Renaissance* 16 (1986): 13–43; and Jean Howard, "The New Historicism in Renaissance Studies," *English Literary Renaissance* 16 (1986): 13–43.

10. Heywood, *An Apology for Actors* (London: Printed by Nicholus Okes, 1612), E 1. See the analysis of Revels Office control over court productions in Richard Dutton, *Mastering the Revels: The Regulation and Censorship of English Renaissance Drama* (Iowa City, 1991); and see also W. R. Streitberger, ed., *Edmond Tyllney, Master of the Revels and Censor of Plays: A Descriptive Index to his Diplomatic Manual on Europe*, (New York, 1986).

11. See Ernest Law, "Shakespeare's 'Tempest' as Originally Produced at Court," (London: De La More Press LTD for the Shakespeare Association, 1923), 5.

12. Quoted in E. K. Chambers, *The Elizabethan Stage*, 4 vols. (Oxford: Oxford University Press, 1923), 1.202–03. See also the full description, with dimensions given, of the Banqueting House and its theatrical equipment in Allardyce Nicoll, *Stuart Masques and the Renaissance Stage* (1938, reprinted, New York, 1963), 32–53.

13. See Jones's drawing (1635) for *Florimène* in the British Library (BL), Lansdowne MS., 1171, ff. 5b, 6.

14. E. K. Chambers, *The Elizabethan Stage*, 2.208.

15. Daniel, *Tethys Festival: or The Queenes wake* (London, printed for John Budge, 1610).

16. See Chambers, *The Elizabethan Stage*, 2.216–17.

17. *Calendar of State Papers, Venetian, 1610–1613*, edited by H. F. Brown (London, 1905), 41, 111.

18. For a discussion of the diplomacy relating to the marriage, see Philippe Erlanger, *L'Empereur Insolite: Rodolphe II de Habsbourg, 1552–1612* (Paris, 1971), 250; Geoffrey Parker, *Europe in Crisis 1589–1648* (London, 1979), 85. Michael Srigley, *Images of Regeneration: A Study of Shakespeare's The Tempest and Its Cultural Background* (Uppsala, 1985), 117–25; and Glynne Wickham, "Masque and Anti-masque in '*The Tempest*'," *Essays and Studies* 28 (1975): 114. See also David M. Bergeron's interpretations of *The Tempest* and related plays in the light of royalist social and political activity in *Shakespeare's Romances and the Royal Family* (Lawrence, Kansas, 1985).

19. See *Works of John Dryden*, eds. Maximillian E. Novak and George Robert Guffey (Berkeley and Los Angeles, 1970), 3. In 1669 Dryden wrote that "The Play itself had formerly been acted with success in the Black-Fryers: and our excellent Fletcher had so great a value for it, that he thought fit to make use of the same Design, no much varied, a second time (3).

20. See Isaacs, *Production and Stage Management at the Blackfriars Playhouse* (1933, reprint, Pennsylvania: Folcroft Library Edition, 1973), 1–28.

21. See Smith's "*The Tempest* as a Kaleidoscope" in *Twentieth Century Interpretation of The Tempest* (Englewood Cliffs, New Jersey, 1969), 3.

22. See T. H. Howard-Hill, ed., *The Tempest: A Concordance to the Text of the First Folio*, (Oxford, 1969), 141–41; and Marvin Spevack, ed., *A Complete and Systematic Concordance to the Works of Shakespeare*, vol. 1 (Hildesheim, 1968), 20. The word "now" is recorded in the concordances as appearing 79 times,

and the word "nows" as appearing once in *The Tempest*.

23. Jonson, *Hymenaei* in *Ben Jonson*, eds. C. H. Herford and Percy and Evelyn Simpson, vol. 7 (1952, reprint Oxford, 1963), 229, ll. 568–79. All line references to Jonson's masques are from this volume.

24. Bergeron in *Shakespeare's Romances* argues that the situation confronting both Alonso, the King of Naples, and Prospero in *The Tempest* was in some ways comparable to the one confronting King James: "Like the royal family in 1611 and 1613, Prospero and Alonso stand ready to give away their royal children in marriage, with all the hopeful prospects that this entails" (203). Bergeron adds that "though Prince Charles remained as heir to the throne, his sickly childhood raised doubts about the possibility of his serving as sovereign" (166–87). Prospero, here seen by Bergeron as mirroring King James giving away the Princess Elizabeth in marriage, is said to grant "Miranda her royal genealogy as he confirms his own in her—again possible succession through the female line. Having gained his crowns through his mother and Princess Margaret, James gives a royal heritage to his children" (193).

25. See the printings of the three plays in *After the Tempest*, edited by George Robert Guffey (Los Angeles, 1969).

Notes to Chapter One

1. T. W. Baldwin, *Shakespeare's Five-Act Structure* (Urbana, Illinois, 1947), 805. See also Baldwin's *Shakespeare's Small Latine and Lesse Greek*, 2 vols. (Urbana, Illinois, 1966); and *On the Literary Genetics of Shakespeare's Plays* (Urbana, Illinois, 1959).

2. R. A. Foakes, *Shakespeare: the Dark Comedies to the Last Plays: from Satire to Celebration* (London, 1971), 144–45. Foakes's study helpfully concentrates upon the play's narrative arrangement and its thematic resemblances to *The Winter's Tale* and *Cymbeline*, but it does not include a formal structural analysis.

3. Heywood, "Of Actors, And the true use of their quality," *An Apologie for Actors* (London: Printed by Nicholas Oakes, 1612), F i.

4. In an early and encompassing study of the degree to which there were or were not act divisions in late sixteenth and early seventeenth century English plays, W. W. Greg in "Act Divisions In Shakespeare," *Review of English Studies* 4 (1928): 157, concludes that "of plays acted by men's companies in the public theatres [1591–1610], the undivided texts are four times as numerous as the divided." A. Quiller-Couch and J. Dover Wilson in

their edition of *The Tempest* (Cambridge, England, 1921) present well-known basic facts and assumptions concerning the "setting out" of the plays in Quarto, noting that "None of the Quartos published during Shakespeare's lifetime contains the conventional divisions which now appear in all modern texts. It would seem, therefore, that he [Shakespeare] did not work in acts and scenes; and the probability that most if not all of these Quartos were printed from prompt-copies suggests that as long as he was at the Globe his plays were performed without breaks." They add that "it seems likely that . . . act divisions are theatrical in origin, and arose from the practice of making four pauses during a performance, which were presumably introduced into Shakespeare's prompt-copies after he had left the Globe" (xxxv–xxxvi). However, T. W. Baldwin in *On Act and Scene Division in the Shakspere First Folio* (Carbondale and Edwardsville, 1965) has maintained on the basis of early composition practice that, although no play manuscripts or play fragments in Shakespeare's hand are extant to provide decisive evidence, "Shakspere constructed in acts and scenes," and that in turn at a later time "the editors for the stage, at least in surviving manuscripts, usually obliterated these markings in manuscript, though making their own annotations . . ." (63). See also the Oxford Press editors Stanley Wells and Gary Taylor, with John Jowett and William Montgomery in *William Shakespeare: A Textual Companion* (Oxford: Oxford University Press, 1947), 1–68; 612–17. Remarking on *The Tempest* in this volume, John Jowett and Stanley Wells suggest that at some period in the presentation of the plays "pauses" were introduced between supposed acts, and that as a result, "F's [Folio's] acts were probably supplied as theatrical act breaks" (p. 612). See also G. K. Hunter, "Structures," Part 3 of *Dramatic Identities and Cultural Tradition: Studies in Shakespeare and his Contemporaries* (New York, 1978), 304–49.

5. Chapman, *The Memorable Masque of the two honourable houses, or Inns of Court, the Middle Temple and Lincoln's Inn* (London: Printed by F. K. for George Norton, no date), C 2, quoted in Stephen Orgel and Roy Strong, eds., *Inigo Jones: Theatre of the Stuart Court*, 2 vols. (Berkeley, 1973), 1.253–63.

6. See Giovanni Battista Guarini, *Il Pastor Fido: Tragi-comedie Pastorale* (London: Giouanni Volfeo, 1591), translated as *Il Pastor Fido: Or The Faithfull Shepheard* (London: Simon Watterson, 1602). See too *A most pleasant Comedie of Mucedorus* (London: Printed for William Iones, 1589); and Samuel Daniel, *The Queenes Arcadia.* A Pastorall Trage-comedie presented to her Maiestie and her Ladies, by the Universitie of Oxford in Christs Church, in August last, 1605. (London: Printed by G. Eld, for Simon

Waterson, 1606). See the later pastoral play by Samuel Daniel, *Hymens Triumph. A Pastorall Tragicomaedie.* Presented at the Queenes Court in the Strand, at her Maiesties magnificent entertainement of the Kings most excellent Maiestie, being at the Nuptials of the Lord Roxborough. (London: Imprinted for Francis Coustable, 1615). See also the suggested background and source works for *The Tempest* appearing in Geoffrey Bullough, ed., *Narrative and Dramatic Sources of Shakespeare,* vol. 8 (London, 1975), 237–423.

7. See Still, *Shakespeare's Mystery Play: A Study of The Tempest* (London, 1921), revised as *The Timeless Theme,* (London, 1936).

8. Srigley, *Images of Regeneration: A Study of Shakespeare's The Tempest and Its Cultural Background* (Uppsala, 1985), 116–66. See also Francis Yates, *The Rosicrucian Enlightenment* (London and Boston, 1972), 57.

9. *Ben Jonson,* 7.211–12, ll. 67–75.

10. *The Rare Triumphs of Loue and Fortune* (London: Printed by E. A. [llde] for Edward White, 1589).

11. See Dominique O. Manmoni's *Prospero and Caliban: The Psychology of Colonization,* trans. Pamela Powesland (New York, 1956). Manmoni, a French psychologist who served briefly as a French government information officer in Madagascar emphasized the actual experience of third world peoples under colonial administrations. This approach stimulated further readings of *The Tempest* from third world perspectives. See also Sibnarayn Ray, "Shylock, Othello and Caliban: Shakespearean Variations on the Theme of Apartheid," *Calcutta Essays on Shakespeare* (Calcutta, 1966), 1–16; and Edward Kamau Brathwaite's "Caliban, Ariel, and Unprospero in the Conflict of Creolization: A Study of the Slave Revolt in Jamaica in 1831–32," *Comparative Perspectives on Slavery in New World Plantation Societies,* eds. Vera Rubin and Arthur Tuden (New York, 1977), 41–62. A series of largely informal essays and stories associating Caliban with oppressed, colonized native populations have been published in a special issue of *The Massachusetts Review* 15 (1973–74).

12. See George Lamming in *The Pleasures of Exile* (London, 1960), 109–10 for a discussion of "linguistic colonialism." Rob Nixon in "Caribbean and African Appropriations of *The Tempest,*" *Critical Inquiry* 8 (1987): 576–78, has taken exception to Lamming's interpretation.

13. Terence Hawkes, *Shakespeare's Talking Animals* (London, 1973).

14. Greenblatt, *Learning to Curse.*

15. See the theoretical and sociological examinations of alleged

colonial references in *The Tempest* in Lorie Leininger, "Cracking the Code of *The Tempest*," *Bucknell Review* 25 (1980): 121–31; Bruce Erlich, "Shakespeare's Colonial Metaphor: On the Social Function of the Theatre in *The Tempest*," *Science and Society* 41 (1977): 43–65; "Hurricanes in the Caribbees: The Constitution of the Discourse of English Colonialism," *1642: Literature and Power in the Seventeenth Century* (1981), 55–83; and Paul N. Seigel, "Historical Ironies in *The Tempest*," *Shakespeare Jahrbuch* 119 (1983): 104–11.

In an example of another kind of theoretical reading, this one in a strain of criticism owing some debts to Frederic Jameson's *The Political Unconscious: Narrative as a Socially Symbolic Act* (Ithaca, New York, 1981), Meredith Anne Skura, in "Discourse and the Individual," puts forward a "colonial" familial reading of *The Tempest* aimed at combining "insights about cultural phenomena like 'power' and 'fields of discourse' and the traditional insights about the text, its immediate sources, its individual author—and his individual psychology" (47). After 24 pages of theoretical analysis of past commentary that includes criticism of Jameson's theory of the collective "political unconscious," Skura simply outlines in three pages some thematic-narrative parallels and contrasts—conveniently calling them "colonial"—so general and metaphoric that both assent and dissent is possible on specific matters. Arguing that "we see Prospero's current relations to Caliban in terms of Prospero's own past," she insists that the play contains "the 'colonial' encounter firmly within the framing story" of the Magus's "own family history." Prospero is said to be "happy in his regressive retreat to his library-Eden; . . . buffered from reality." "Only when Antonio's betrayal," Skura writes, shattered Prospero's trust and cast him "from Eden—newly aware of both the brother as Other and himself as a willful self in opposition—did he 'discover' the island and Caliban. In a sense, then, Caliban emerged from the rift between Prospero and Antonio ." A "'colonialist' Prospero" then imposes," according to Skura, a "distance" between "self and Other." "When Prospero acknowledges Caliban," she concludes, "he thus partly defuses an entire dynamic that began long before he had ever seen the island" (66).

16. Hamilton, *Virgil and The Tempest: The Politics of Imitation* (Columbus, Ohio, 1989), 17. See also Hamilton, *Shakespeare and the Politics of Protestant England* (New York, 1992).

17. *The whole xii Bookes of the Aeneidos of Virgill*, trans. Thoman Phaer with Thomas Twyne (London: Wyllyam How, 1573), with book divisions, but unpaginated and without numbered lines. The harpy reference in book 3 is by line count l. 226.

18. Hamilton in *Virgil and The Tempest*, for example, writes in free-associative fashion that

> As a magus, Prospero is like a god, a first mover; he makes and unmakes all the situations of the island. He also takes it for granted that Ariel and Caliban should serve him (supply him), that they should be punished if they complain, perhaps even silenced. . . . Ariel serves an apprenticeship; Caliban has been made a prisoner. At times Ariel seems to reflect the king's faithful followers, at others, he exhibits the formally obsequious behavior that even a distraught Commons would use when confronting the king. Likewise, Caliban images the displanted native of Virginia or Ireland, but also the English fear of being made "slaves" in their own land. Whatever the case, together these characters represent the issues of service and supply, restraint and complaint from different angles, which, in combination and in juxtaposition, present a complex and provocative picture of issues of reciprocity as they were being debated at this time (53–54).

19. See Baltasar de Beaujoyeulx, *Balet Comique de la Royne* (Paris: Imprimeurs du Roy, 1582); the *Proteus* masque in John Nichols, *The Progresses and Public Processions of Queen Elizabeth I*, vol. 1 (London, 1828): 281–82; W. W. Greg, ed., *Gesta Grayorum*, (1688; reprint, Oxford, 1914), x–xx; *The Inner Temple Masque* in *Poems of William Browne of Tavistock*, ed. Gordon Goodwin, vol. 2 (London, 1905); and *A Masque Presented at Ludlow Castle* in *John Milton: Complete Poetry and Minor Prose*, ed. Merritt Y. Hughes (Indianapolis, 1957). The masque is explicated in the light of European spectacle iconography in John Demaray, "The Temple of the Mind: Cosmic Iconography" in *Milton's A Mask, Comus Contexts*, ed. Roy Flannagan (Binghamton, New York, 1988), 59–76.

20. For an analysis of European academies and their theatrical theories, see Francis Yates, *The French Academies of the Sixteenth Century* (London, 1947). For critiques of the nature and history of French spectacle triumphs, see Paul Lacroix, *Ballets et Mascarades de Cour de Henri III a Louis XIV*, 5 vols. (Paris, 1868); and J. Chartrou, *Les Entries solennelles et triomphales à la Renaissance* (Paris, 1928). It should be noted that the copy of the influential *Balet Comique de la Royne* owned and marked in the margins by Ben Jonson is in the collection of the New York Public Library. The *Balet*, about the enchantments of Circe, was directly imitated in England by Aurelian Townshend in *Tempe Restored* (1632).

21. James I, *Daemonologie, in forme of a Dialogue* (1597: reprint London, 1924).

22. *The xv. Bookes of P. Ovidius Naso, entyuled Metamorphosis, translated oute of Latin into English meeter, by Arthur Golding Gentleman*, (London: Willyam Seres, 1571), 87–92. The lines are unnumbered, but references are here given by a line count. See also the Medea and Jason passion narrative in *Apollonii Rhodii Argonavticorvm*, Greek text with accompanying Latin trans. by Jeremia Hoelzlino (Lugduno-Batavae, 1641), 3.270–323, ll. 33–666; 3.344–50, ll. 970–1007.

23. See also Elizabeth Truax, *Metamorphosis in Shakespeare's Plays: A Pageant of Heroes, Gods, Maids and Monsters*, (Lewiston, 1992). Although Truax focuses on Shakespearean plays other than *The Tempest*, she demonstrates the strong, general influence of Ovid's *Metamorphoses* upon the playwright; and she argues that Shakespeare's use of theatrical icons—icons that she finds derived in part from court masques—"transcend the limitations of genres." Truax also helpfully calls attention to the choreographic nature of Shakespeare's iconography. "Working hand in hand with Nature," she writes, "Shakespeare creates an art of the theatre that fuses the painter's imitation of bodily form, movement and gesture with the poet's language to create stage pictures that lay bare the deepest truths of human experience . . ." (12).

24. Kermode, *The Tempest: the Arden Edition*, xxiv.

25. Welsford, *The Court Masque* (Cambridge, England, 1927), 340.

26. *The Works of Samuel Johnson*, ed. F. P. Walesbay, vol. 7 (Oxford, 1825): 123.

27. Ronald Bayne, "Masque and Pastoral," chap. 13 in *The Cambridge History of English Literature*, eds. A. W. Ward and A. R. Waller, vol. 6 (1910: reprint Cambridge, England, 1919): 363.

28. See the first 1637 edition of *A Mask Presented at Ludlow Castle* in *John Milton*, 112.

29. For a structural analysis of the masque with stress upon the work's pervasive choreographic symbolism, see Demaray, *Milton and the Masque Tradition* (Cambridge, Massachusetts: 1968), 92–121; and "The Temple of the Mind," *Comus Contexts*, 59–76.

30. Kermode, *The Tempest: the Arden Edition*, lxxiv, n. 3. Kermode in note 2 on the same page records an insightful structural suggestion from D. J. Gordon: "that at the climax of each plot there is a spectacular contrivance borrowed from the masque: thus the rapacity of the 'men of sin' is confronted with its own image in the Harpy; the disorderly desires of Caliban and the rest are chastised by hounds who, in the Actaeon story, typify such

desires; and the betrothal of Miranda is conventionally signalized by a courtly mythological entertainment."

31. Frank Kermode, *Shakespeare: The Final Plays*, (London, 1963–65), 43–44.

32. Robert Grudin, "Prospero's Masque and the Structure of *The Tempest*," *The South Atlantic Quarterly* 71 (Winter, 1972): 405.

33. Wickham, "Masque and Anti-masque," 2–5.

34. Ernest B. Gilman, "'All Eyes': Prospero's Inverted Masque," *Renaissance Quarterly* 33 (1980), 215. See also Kevin R. McNamara in "Golden Worlds at Court: *The Tempest* and its Masque," *Shakespeare Studies* 19 (1987): 183–202, which combines Gilman's comments on the fourth-act dissolution of the revels with Kermode's neo-Terentian structural analysis to transform the play into a supposedly "tragic" work. Also see Peter Holland, "The Shapeliness of *The Tempest*," *Essays in Criticism* XLV, no. 3 (July, 1995): 208–29. Holland has turned to Mark Rose's *Shakespearean Design* (Cambridge, Massachusetts, 1972) to suggest that Shakespeare used groups of characters as framing devices.

Notes to Chapter Two

1. *Hall's Chronicle* 3 (1809): 40. See also Edward Hall, *The Union of the two noble and illustre famelies of Lancastre & Yorke*, (London: R. Graftoni, 1548).

2. See John Nichols's *The Progresses and Public Processions of Queen Elizabeth*, vol. 1, (London, 1823): 429ff.

3. Roy Strong, *Splendor at Court: Renaissance Spectacle and the Theater of Power* (Boston: 1973), 54, 144–67.

4. Baltasar de Beaujoyeulx, *Balet Comique de la Royne* (Paris: Imprimeurs du Roy, 1582).

5. The ballets appear respectively in Paul Lacroix, *Ballets et Mascarades de Cour: 1581–1652*, vol. 2 (Geneve, 1868), l. 117–34, 163–98; 2. 1–9, 28–35, 163–198, 14–23. See Henry Prunieres, *Le Ballet de cour en France avant Benserade et Lully* vol. 1 (Paris 1914) and the related *L'Opera Italien en France avant Lulli* (Paris, 1913). See also J. Chartrou, *Les Entriés solennelles et triomphales à la Renaissance* (Paris, 1920). The varied character-types in the spectacle productions are discussed in La Laurencie, *Les createurs de l'opera francais* (Paris, 1921).

6. See the discussion of influence of the French court theatrical tradition on Shakespeare in Frances Yates, *A Study of Love's Labour's Lost* (Cambridge, England, 1936). See also Erica Veevers,

Images of Love and Religion: Queen Henrietta Maria and Court Entertainments (Cambridge, England, 1989).

7. *Ben Jonson* 7.282, ll. 10–14.

8. See the quotation of Henrietta Maria in Nicoll, *Stuart Masques*, 116.

9. The *Expostulation* lines are quoted in Enid Welsford, *The Court Masque*, 218.

10. *John Milton*, 96, ll. 245, 267; 97, ll. 298–90.

11. Miranda is correct in asserting that Caliban's punishment has actually been quite mild:

> . . . thy vild race
> (Tho thou didst learn) had that in't, which good natures
> Could not abide to be with; therefore wast thou
> Deseruedly confin'd into this Rocke, who hadst
> Deseru'd more than a prison.
>
> (D. 5)

Although Prospero verbally castigates Caliban and calls the creature one "Whom stripes may moue, not kindnes" (D. 5), the enchanter actually metes out relatively restrained chastisement of a practical or imaginative kind. Prospero forces the monster to carry logs while threatening Caliban with fanciful harms appropriate to faeries: "cramps,/Side-stiches, that shall pen thy breath vp" (D. 4); "thou shalt be pinch'd,/As thicke as hony-combe, each pinch more stinging/ Then Bees that made 'em" (D. 4).

Notes to Chapter Three

1. Gerald Eades Bentley, "Shakespeare and the Blackfriars Theatre," *Shakespeare Survey* 1 (1948): 38–50. Bentley, in discussing plays presented at the Blackfriars, explains what he would have argued had he been "participating in the conferences about the Blackfriars" with the King's men (44). The essay was revised and reprinted as the chapter "Shakespeare and the Blackfriars Theatre" in *Shakespeare and His Theatre* (Lincoln, Nebraska, 1964).

Bentley's views were a response to earlier general commentary such as that by Ernest Law who, in the Shakespeare Association Pamphlet *Shakespeare's 'Tempest' as Originally Produced at Court* (1920), maintained the play would have been presented at Whitehall like a masque. For a seminal scholarly discussion of Shakespearean productions at Blackfriars, see Issacs, Shakespeare Association Pamphlet, *Production and Stage Management at the Blackfriars Theatre.*

2. See E. K. Chambers, *William Shakespeare,* 2.342 (Revels Account) and 343 (Chambers Account). The Revels Account of 1611 notes that on "Hollowmas nyght was presented at Whitehall before the Kinges Maiestie a play Called the Tempest." Two years later, a Chambers Account contains an "Item paid to John Heminges . . . dated att Whitehall xx die Maij 1613, for presentinge before the Princes Highnes the Lady Elizabeth and the Prince Pallatyne Elector . . . The Tempest."

Evidence suggests the 1611 presentation was in the Banqueting House. The Audit Office Declared Accounts for October 1611 note a payment "To James Maxwell gentleman usher . . . for making ready . . . the Banqueting House there three severall tymes for playes . . ." (PRO, Declared Account, Bundle 389, Roll 49, fol. 10b); and in late October and early November, the King's Men were paid for the Whitehall performances of three plays: *The Tempest, The Winter's Tale* and a third drama.

3. See Chambers, *The Elizabethan Stage* 2.216–17.

4. See John Long, *Shakespeare's Use of Music: The Final Comedies* (Gainesville, 1961), 115–24; and A. M. Nagler, *Shakespeare's Stage* (New Haven, 1973), 104–07.

5. For an analysis of courtly stage arrangements in Europe, Whitehall, and at aristocratic functions outside London, see Nicoll, *Stuart Masques,* 28–53; John Orrell, *The Human Stage: English Theatre Design, 1567–1640* (Cambridge, England, 1988), *The Theatres of Inigo Jones and John Webb* (Cambridge, England, 1985); and John G. Demaray, *Milton and the Masque Tradition;* "Milton's Comus: The Sequel to a Masque of Circe," *The Huntington Library Quarterly* (May, 1966): 245–54; and *Milton's Theatrical Epic* (Cambridge, Massachusetts, 1980), 35–43. See also David More Bergeron, ed., *Pageantry in the Shakespearean Theatre,* (Athens, Georgia, 1985); and Bergeron's *English Civic Pageantry: 1558–1642* (London: 1971).

At the English court in the early seventeenth century, royal celebratory presentations were regularly staged in the rectangular Whitehall Masquing House, and on some occasions, in the rectangular Grand Chamber. In both of these halls during the 1611–13 period, as noted, the stage with proscenium arch and curtain was placed at a narrow end of the chamber, the aristocratic audience was placed on three sides against the walls, and the king uplifted on a platform "in state" in the rear-center but away from the walls. A smaller chamber, the semicircular Cockpit at Court was sometimes used for informal theatrical presentations, but it was not customarily used for ceremonial royal productions before the full court.

See Nicoll, 32–53, for accounts of primary documents giving a ground plan of the Old Masquing House, built in 1581 and reconstructed in 1606, and its arrangement for theatrical presentations with seats, stage, proscenium arch, royal platform, and open dancing space. See also Inigo Jones' drawing (1635) of the ground plan and staging arrangements for the French pastoral *Florimène*, a drawing showing the New Masquing House of 1622 reconstructed in the form of the Old, with the same staging arrangement as that used for masques (BL, Lansdowne MS, 1171, ff. 5b, 6). E. K. Chambers in *The Elizabethan Stage* l. 202–03, authoritatively discusses the Hall and quotes early descriptions, by John Finett in 1616 and Orazio Busino in 1618, of its arrangement for theatrical presentations. See also Gerald Eades Bentley, *The Jacobean and Caroline Stage*, vol. 6 (Oxford, 1968): 255–84, for accounts from primary documents of the Cockpit-at-Court and the court Grand Chamber.

Although Leslie Hotson has argued in *The First Night of Twelfth Night* (New York, 1954), that this individual play, unlike others, was presented in the Grand Chamber "in-the-round" with the stage at the hall's center, Hotson's interpretation is at variance with existing elevation sketches for court productions at Whitehall, and with wider traditional court stage arrangements of this period employed in Paris and Florence as well as in London. As A. M. Nagler notes in *Shakespeare's Stage*, enlarged ed. (New Haven, 1981), Hotson "based his theory" on a letter in which Don Virginio Orsini, Duke of Bracciano, states that at the first production of *Twelfth Night*, "the ladies had sat on *gradi* which were disposed "*Atorno atorno*," the last words taken literally as meaning "on all four sides" (39). Nagler rightly takes exception to this interpretation, pointing out that "Bastiano de' Rossi, in his account of *Amico fido* as staged by Bernardo Buontalenti at the Ufizzi Theatre in 1585–86, relates that "the ladies sat on gradi which surrounded the hall *intorno intorno*. We know that the *gradi* were not on all four sides: for Buontalenti's stage was situated on the fourth side. Thus the repetition of *atorno* or *intorno* meant nothing more than on three sides" (39–40).

6. If Shakespeare introduced the Folio act divisions and intended a performance "pause" between acts 4 and 5—that point at which Prospero and Ariel exit and reenter, and the Magus puts on his "*magick robes*"—then it is entirely possible that these actions were included to allow for a between-acts musical interlude and costume change of a sort popular at Blackfriars. But given Whitehall staging, and given the high probability that Shakespeare neither inserted the act divisions nor anticipated a "pause" at this point, the actions of Prospero and Ariel can also be seen as reflecting court staging traditions, specifically the court masque

ritualistic convention of the "donning" and "doffing" of sequined robes to symbolize changes in the relation of featured performers to cosmic forces. Prospero assumes and removes his magical robes in act 1. Then Trincolo and Stephano in act 4, in a parody of true "enrobement," briefly don the Magus's "*glistering* apparell" after entering and leaving Prospero's Cell. Finally, Ariel and Prospero enter the Cell at the "apex" of the Magus's power so that Prospero can don his sparkling robes for the last time, most probably at center stage in full view of the court audience. Prospero would then, without pause, step forward, very likely holding the magic staff and book which he mentions in his famous act 5 speech on magic.

As Grace Ioppolo has pointed out in *Revising Shakespeare* (Cambridge, Massachusetts, 1991), 205, n. 53, the actual text of the *The Tempest*, was not printed in quarto and shows no evidence of "demonstrable authorial revision." She appropriately finds it among those Shakespearean dramas that do not require editorial reconstruction, although she writes in favor of such reconstruction when variant texts are extant.

7. See Nicola Sabbattini on the placement of the "Principe" in *Pratica Di Fabricar Scene, E Machine* (Ravenna: Per Pietro de' Paoli, e Gio. Battista Giouannelli, 1638), 55. See also the accounts of the king's uplifted platform in relation to the stage and to the seated aristocrats in Bentley, *The Jacobean and Caroline Stage*, 255–84; Nicoll, *Stuart Masques*, 28–53; and Demaray, *Milton and the Masque Tradition*, 33–39.

8. *Ben Jonson*, 7.488, ll. 261–666; 489, l. 282.

9. Gurr, "*The Tempest*'s Tempest at Blackfriars," *Shakespeare Survey* 41 (1989): 94. See also D. 4.

10. *John Milton*, 82–83, l. 219.

11. Gurr, "The Tempest's Tempest at Blackfriars," 91–102. See also Irwin Smith, "Ariel and the Masque in *The Tempest*," *Shakespeare Quarterly* 21 (1970): 213–22.

12. See F. W. Sternfield, *Music in Shakespearean Tragedy* (London, 1963), 80; and John Long, *Shakespeare's Use of Music* (Gainesville, Florida, 1961), 113.

13. *The discouerie of witchcraft* (n.p., 1584), 350–52. The illustration shows the top of a table, with a hole at its center, cut down the middle lengthwise so that the two sections or, more likely, just the rear section can be slid open.

14. See the commentary on *The Tempest* by John Jowett and Stanley Wells in the volume collectively written by Wells et al., *William Shakespeare: A Textual Companion*, 612. Jowett and Wells rightly observe that the textual problem of the "*Juno descends*" stage direction is not "touched" by the issue of whether

the masque might have been "interpolated," that is, inserted into the text for the play's performance in 1613 at Whitehall on the occasion of the marriage of Princess Elizabeth to the Elector Palatine. See note 16 for Jowett and Orgel's interpretation of the "Juno descends" stage direction.

In an early, highly hypothetical study, D. Grey, in *Studies in Philology* 18 (1921): 129, argues that the betrothal masque and the "masque" of dogs in act 4, together with other passages in the act, were interpolated for the 1613 performance. Grey then makes an imaginative effort to fill up the act with the kind of action that he assumes would have been there for the 1611 presentation. Recently, Irwin Smith in "Ariel and the Masque in *The Tempest*," *Shakespeare Quarterly* 21 (1970): 213–22, has revived Grey's view, with which most critics and scholars have disagreed, that the betrothal masque in act 4 was a late "insert" into the 1613 version. His highly speculative reading, resting in considerable measure on a nontraditional interpretation of the masquing term "presented," does helpfully call attention to possible Whitehall staging in 1613 in the open center of the hall; but is otherwise unconvincing because it lacks references to overall thematic elements and to key conventions of court production. The basic case for the thematic and contextual appropriateness of the betrothal masque, against claims that components of the masque are late insertions, has been effectively advanced by, among others, E. K. Chambers in *Shakespearean Gleanings* (London, 1944), 77–80, 88–92.

15. See the Oxford Shakespeare edition of *The Tempest*, ed. Orgel (Oxford: 1987), 3, and Kermode *The Tempest: The Arden Edition*, 152–53.

The stage direction "*Juno descends*" is altered from that in the 1623 Folio, usually with other directions by editors added, in almost all modern editions of *The Tempest*, including those by David Bevington, Northrop Frye, Alfred Harbage, G. B. Harrison, George Lyman Kittredge, Irving Ribner, J. Dover Wilson and Arthur Quiller-Couch and William Aldis Wright.

Orgel maintains, however, that even the presence in *The Tempest* of allusions to a wedding masque, of a kind regularly presented at court, "is no evidence that a courtly venue was intended, and in this case it may, in fact, imply just the reverse: the mechanics of the masque and the apparitions in *The Tempest* are those of the public theatre—descents and ascents, properties appearing and disappearing through trapdoors—not those of the Banqueting House, with its changeable scenery" (2). Similarly, Frank Kermode insists that "the Globe had the three-level tiring-house which seems indispensible, as well as the necessary traps and machines to deal with the more spectacular episodes." He finds the views of John Cranford Adams "surely incontrovertible in his insistence on the importance of the Globe's mechanical apparatus." And though Kermode notes that "the play could easily have been acted at both Blackfriars and the Globe," he concludes that, because of its capability for "more subtle effects . . . the Blackfriars was the natural home of the play" (152–53). Kermode is unusual as an editor, however, in that he retains the basic Folio stage directions while interpolating his own directions signifying the place where each scene unfolds.

The "incontrovertable" positions of John Cranford Adams in *The Globe Playhouse: Its Design and Equipment* (New York, 1961) are, in fact, extremely tenuous because extant public theatre records on staging are few as compared to those extant for the court. Lacking English public theatre precedents for Ariel's "flight," for example, Adams insists that this "flight"—which is not mentioned in the Folio stage directions which read simply "*Enter Ariell*" (D. 13)—must have been staged experimentally. Adam surmises and then states categorically that "Ariel's descent . . . was the first 'free flight' in the history of the English public stage. Thereafter, actors can 'fly' down from the heavens without any other apparatus than some sort of belt or harness (concealed beneath their costumes?) to which a wire was attached" (339). For recent commentary on the stage and stage effects at the Globe, see Stanley Wells, "Staging Shakespeare's Apparitions and Dream Visions, *The First Annual Shakespeare Globe Lecture*, (London, 1995); and "Shakespeare's Globe: Evaluating the archaeological evidence from the 1989 and 1992 digs at the site of the Globe," *Antiquity* 66 (June, 1992): 315–33.

16. Orgel, *The Tempest*, 2. Orgel states that he is "wholly convinced" (175, n. 74.1) by the flight analysis of theatre historian John Jowett in "New Created Creatures: Ralph Crane and the Stage Directions in '*The Tempest*,' *Shakespeare Survey* 36 (1963): 107–20. Jowett goes well beyond Folio textual references by assuming that Juno would be lowered on wires in a chariot, which Jowett later calls a throne, at the stage direction "*Juno descends*," and then, perhaps together with Ceres, "would be rapidly pulled up to the heavens when the spirits 'vanish.'" Jowett theorizes that Juno would descend beginning 1.74 to a "stationary position in the air" in accord with what he calls "the convention of the floating deity" (116–17); but he does not explain how Juno would remain "stationary" while dangling from wires that have a tendency to swing figures back and forth. Orgel, in his own inserted directions also describes a chariot, not mentioned in any printing of the folio text, in recording the descent of Juno. He

then adds another of his own stage directions to the text by writing in the chariot's landing. Finally, he interpolates an upward flight back to the heavens by Ceres and Juno that neither appears in nor is implied in the text, but which rather arises from Jowett's staging assumptions. Orgel's added stage direction reads: "*Ceres joins Juno in the chariot, which rises and hovers above the stage*" (*The Tempest*, 177).

Jowett does sound a much-needed cautionary note in arguing for this nontextual, excessively prolonged, and amateurish dangling-wire-type suspension: "The throne may require some careful balancing or extra wires to take first one, than two characters" ("New Created Creatures," 117).

In a handsome compilation of masque designs reproduced with the full texts of masques, *Inigo Jones: The Theatre of the Stuart Court*, editors Orgel and Roy Strong analyze Inigo Jones's drawings with special attention to the iconography and to certain illustrated stage effects. But in regard to early masques such as *Hymenaei* (1606), *Lord Haye's Masque* (1607), the *Lords Masque* (1613) and the *Inner Temple Masque* (1613), they make no editorial comment on the possible operation of the levitation and descent machines, or of the stage-level lowering and raising of performers described in the masques' stage directions. These omissions, I think, lead to some confusion about the nature and apparently, even about the existence of the effects. The editors, as a stated policy, comment on "Jones's engineering" only when stage effects described in masque texts are accompanied by drawings or early notations offering particular information on the operation of the specific stage devices employed (18).

In their introduction, Orgel and Strong make a brief remark on levitations and descents in relation to a so-called Whitehall "fly gallery," also referred to by Orgel in his Arden *Tempest* edition. Writing generally of masque "aerial" stage effects, the editors state that in court masques, "extensive arial spectacles were achieved only after Jones's stage included a fly gallery about 1631," a gallery here defined as a "separate playing area" in the "heavens," and as a "tiered upper stage" illustrated in the "side elevation" for the pastoral drama *Florimème* (18). But this kind of playing area in the heavens was in evidence many years earlier for the production of *Hymenae* and other court masques and even then used to achieve "aerial spectacles" that in later years became more lavish. Moreover, there is no evidence that it was used even in later years on the Whitehall stage, as Orgel implies in the Arden edition, to lower performers dangling on a wire. The editors even appear to reverse their views on the "new" Whitehall fly gallery when, a few lines after first mentioning it, they observe that "such a structure must have been in use twenty years earlier, e.g. for the Temple of Fame in Chapman's 1613 masque, and Campion actually refers to it when he says that the scene of the *Lords Masque* in the same year 'was divided in two parts from the roof to the floor'" (18).

See also Allardyce Nicoll who in *Stuart Masques*, 63–77, records and comments upon the numerous cloud "descents" and levitations on the Whitehall masquing stage in the 1608–13 period, including those in *Hymenaei*, and who traces and speculates upon the Italian origins of the post-and-beam machines that were used by Jones in creating these Whitehall levitation effects.

17. Roger Warren, *Staging Shakespeare's Late Plays* (Oxford, 1990), 192.

18. T. W. Baldwin in *On Act and Scene Division in the Shakspere First Folio* (Carbondale and Edwardsville, 1965), presents reasonable and well-known basic assumptions in arguing that *The Tempest*, because it was printed in a relatively finished form without serious gaps or disrceprencies, "might be derived from . . . Prompt Books" (154). This view has been advanced by many commentators, including John Dover Wilson and Arthur Quiller-Couch in their Cambridge edition of *The Tempest* (London, New York, Melbourne, 1977; reprinted from the 1921 edition), xxxv–xxxvi; and by John Jowett and Stanley Wells in *William Shakespeare: A Textual Companion*, 612. John Dover Wilson, moreover, maintains in the Cambridge edition of the play that the stage directions in the 1623 Folio text were written by Shakespeare, and then possibly abridged by him in semi-retirement (80).

On the other hand, John Jowett and Stanley Wells claim to detect, largely on very slender "stylistic evidence . . . two strata of directions," one by Shakespeare and another by a second hand identified as probably that of Ralph Crane.

The problem with this position is that Jowett and Wells cannot convincingly delineate the work of the "second hand," for they add that the "strata" are so intermeshed that they "cannot be clinically separated." The words and phrases that they suggest "might have been written by Crane," all cited from stage directions, are not sufficiently distinctive to give adequate weight to their assertions. The cited words and phrases could well have been written by Shakespeare to supplement allusions in the dialogue of the play to stage and scenic effects; namely, "*A tempestuous noise*" (1.1.0.1/0.1), "*confused*" (1.1.57/59), "*dispersedly*" (1.2.385/451), "*shapes*" (3.3.18.1/1366.1 and (3.3.82.2/1429.2), "*with gentle actions of salutations*" (33.3.18.2–3/1366.2–3), "*with a quient device*" (3.3.52.3–4/1399.3/1399.3–4), "*properly habited*"

(4.1.138.1/1594.1) and *"a strange hollow and confused noyse"* (4.1.142.1/1598.1) (612). Even if it is assumed that the stage directions were in part written by Crane or someone else, the directions may well have mirrored the second writer's memory of early productions.

19. *Ben Jonson*, 7.232, ll. 666–67.

In Thomas Campion's *Lords Masque* (London: Printed for John Budge, 1613) and Francis Beaumont's *Inner Temple Masque* (London: Imprinted by F. K. for George Norton, 1613), presented respectively on 14 February and 20 February 1613 at the Banqueting House just before the presentation of *The Tempest*, a total of 14 persons floated down from the heavens on clouds. That year there was no lack of expertise for Juno's descent. *"Master* Innigoe Jones," writes Campion in his stage directions for the *Lords Masque, "in the workmanship which belong'd to the whole inuention, shewed extraordinarie industrie and skill"* (page unnumbered).

20. For the 17 handwritten parchment Lord Chamberlain's Rolls for 1603 through 1638, see the British Public Records Office collection, E 351–2805.

21. See Sabbattini, *Pratica Di Fabricar Scene*, 135–37. The stage-section drawing for *Salmacida Spoila* showing the rear-center suspension machine is in the British Library, Ms. Lansdowne, 1171, ff. Ib–2. The drawing also shows two upright posts placed behind side-shutters for use in lowering figures to the stage. The drawing is reproduced in Nicoll, *Stuart Masques*, 121, Fig. 79; and Orgel and Strong, eds., in *Inigo Jones*, 2.740–41, sketch 400. By contrast, see the discussion of English public theatre dangling-from-a-rope flight machines, with an illustration of an Italian model of this type, in C. Walter Hodges, *The Globe Restored*, (New York: 1653), 117, 161. See also the study of the public theatre machines in John H. Astington's "Descent Machinery in the Playhouses," *Medieval & Renaissance Drama in England* 2, (1985): 119–33, which includes illustrations of both dangling-rope devices and the Whitehall machine used in *Salmacida Spolia.*

22. *Documents Relating to the Office of the Revels in the Time of Queen Elizabeth*, ed. A. Feuillerat, *Materialien zur Kunde des alteren Englischen Dramas*, vol. 21 (Louvain, 1914), 227. The Revels Accounts also show that property-maker "John Rosse" was twice paid for the construction of floating clouds in 1575, for "Long boordes for the Stere of a clowde," and for "Pulleys for the Clowdes"; and in 1578 for "nayles of sundry sortes vsed about the Clowde for drawing it upp and downe" (240, 308).

23. See Sabbattini, *Pratica Di Fabricar Scene*, 135–56, for

comments on various types of cloud and levitation devices, with the stirrup device described in chapter 50. None of the court levitation machines that Sabbattini discusses employ the public theatre method of lowering figures on a visible rope.

24. PRO Roll Listing Expenses for 1611–1612, E 351–2805.

25. In commenting upon the possible stage setting for just the 1613 court mounting of *The Tempest*, John Long in *Shakespeare's Use of Music*, 115–24, gives the impression that in 1613 levitation machines were not available, and that Juno would have had to walk down from above—a view once suggested by E. Law—rather than "descend" in flight in traditional fashion. Long points out that in the staging of Thomas Campion's *Lords Masque* in the Banqueting House on 14 February 1613, a ramp was used between upper and lower stage levels. He then states that this setting, showing a cave stage left and a mountain stage center, might have been used again without alteration for *The Tempest*; and that in the 1613 Whitehall presentation of Shakespeare's play, Juno appears "from behind the mountain-top of the upper scene" and walks "by a ramp or stairway to the middle scene," before finally pacing down to the stage. In act 1, scene 2, Long notes that Ferdinand and Miranda would be "seated in front of the cave at the left side" (115). He similarly places other action before the cell at stage left.

Long does not note that the "Cave" on the Banqueting House stage for the *Lords Masque* was the abode of the antic figure "Mania," who dances discordantly with the wild "Frantics." The "Cave" was accordingly located in a negative or antic position, "On the left hand," when viewed from the seat of state. Featured virtuous figures, by contrast, traditionally had their "seats" or "cells" center stage. Nor does Long refer to any of the court levitation machine descents which, in the year 1613, alone floated 20 persons to the court stage. In the *Lord's Masque* itself, the main "*eight Maskers appeared*" on what was obviously the center upper-level stage when eight "*Starres suddainely vanished, as if they had beene drowned amongst the Cloudes.*" The masquers then descended by means of a levitation machine on a "bright and transparant cloud"; and "*at the end of their descent, the cloud brake in twaine, and one part of it (as with a winde) was blowne ouerthwart the Scene.*"

26. Orgel, in the introduction to his edition, suggests the allusion to the green could refer to "the Blackfriars, where the stage was covered with fresh green rushes, and may also have been appropriate to a production at the Globe" (2–3). This alternative reading seems somewhat strained. Given the context of the known productions of the play at Whitehall, "green"—appearing

as it does in the masque in act 4 amid allusions to a masque dance by rural figures and to Juno's long masquing descent and special masquing "gait" (D. 14)—quite directly suggests, among its meanings, the artificial "green" or rug on which performers regularly paced and danced at court.

27. *The Description of a Maske, Presented before the Kinges Maiestie at White-Hall, on Twelfth Night last, in honour of the Lord Hayes.* (S. Dunstones Churchyeard in Fleetstreet, London, 1607), C3–D2. See also *The Description of a Maske* in *Campion's Works*, ed. Percival Vivian (Oxford, 1909), 70–71.

28. See *The Triumph of Peace* in *James Shirley* (London, 1927), 462–63.

29. *John Milton*, 44, ll. 47–50. See also how the figure Sabrina in *A Mask Presented at Ludlow Castle*, obviously making an entrance from below stage on a machine moving upward in groves, "rises" in a "sliding Chariot" (111, ll. 888, 892).

30. See Milbourne Christopher, *The Illustrated History of Magic*, (New York, 1973), 157–72.

31. See Sabbattini, *Pratica Di Fabricar Scene*, 71–72, for a discussion of the operation of the shutters and the method of misdirection. In his final designs for Oberon staged on 1 January 1611, Inigo Jones included layered shutters that could be quickly "pulled" in grooves to change scenes, a method he continued to use in later masques. In *Hymenaei* (1606) and *Queenes* (1609), Jones made upstage-center scenic changes by revolving devices and flats on some kind of pivot or platform framed by regular flats. Allardyce Nicoll in *Stuart Masques*, 63–67, maintains that Jones rapidly changed scenes in *Queenes* possibly by having flats pulled—the term "cleave," for example, appears in the description of a cliff that opens—or by employing rows of pivots in some locations in the form of triangular, simultaneously turned pillars, *periaktoi*, with different scenes painted on each side.

See Nicoll's *Stuart Masques*, 63ff. and *The Development of the Theatre*, 5th ed. (London, 1966), 106ff., for an assessment of English court scene changes in the light of Italian and European practices. See also Orgel and Strong in *Inigo Jones*, 1.105ff., for accounts of Jones's designs for center-stage scene changes using a *machina versatilis* in *Hymenaei* and *Queenes*, and for the employment of pulled, layered flats in *Oberon* and later masques. Yet to be fully analyzed is precisely how Jones designed and operated the center-stage pivoting globe in *Hymenaei* which, according to John Porey, "hung, or rather stood (for no axle was seen to support it)," (*Ben Jonson*, 10.465–680). See too James J. Yoch, Jr., "Subjecting the Landscape in Pageants and Shakespearean Pastorals," and David Moore Beregeron, ed., *Pageantry in Shakespearean Theatre,* (Athens, Georgia, 1985), 194–219, for an examination of scenic and landscape references in *The Tempest* in relation to stage and actual garden designs.

32. To mount the opening scene showing a ship in a storm, the Office could have used selected scenic elements from the beginning of Daniel's *Tethy's Festival* (London: Printed for John Budge, 1610), p. unnumbered, showing "Ships . . . some neerer and some further off" that "seemed to mooue with a gentle gale"; or from the opening of Jonson's *The Masque of Blackness* (1605) in which a wavering "artificiall sea" supported masquers who were encompassed in a great "shell" that was "curiously made to moue on those waters, and move with the billow" (ll. 26, 59–61). See also Sabbattini, *Practica Di Fabricar Scene,* 107–33, for sea and ship effects; and for lighting and thunder effects, 156–58.

A. M. Nagler in *Shakespeare's Stage,* placing emphasis on possible Blackfriars productions of the play, maintains rather impressionistically that the "superfluous" shipwreck scene would have been "deleted at Court," a view that seems to me misguided because it is based on literalist medieval rather than iconographic Jacobean stagecraft. "The producers," Nagler writes, would not "roll a three-dimensional ship on stage (although that would not have been difficult for the stage technicians of the time, since ships had already been used in medieval mystery plays)." Nagler does raise the possibility that, at Whitehall, "the King's Men played on a proscenium-frame stage with a cave for Caliban, grass mats and palm trees to bring out the exotic atmosphere of the island, and a rocklike built piece hallowed out to provide a cell for Prospero" (104–05). Nagler does not, however, discuss "vanishes" or "descents."

Kevin R. McNamara in "Golden Worlds at Court," 183–202, bases a very different and largely impressionistic staging analysis on the hypothesis that "this play was written for performance in a private theatre" (184). Consequently, he imagines and describes a generally "bare stage" production, with scenery and stage machinery introduced for the betrothal masque. Accepting Ernest B. Gilman's reading of a theatrical "pivotal point" at the end of act 4, and also Frank Kermode's positing of a "Neo-Terentian" structure, McNamara, I think, exaggerates what he calls the dramatic motive of this very ritualistic work by finding Prospero's situation "tragic" after the dissolution of the masque. "The 'tragic' moment, he writes, "is the play's rejection of the masque's simple answers" (198).

33. *Loves Crveltie. A Tragedy* (London: Printed by Tho. Cotes, for Andrew Crooke, 1640), D, Bridgewater Library copy, Huntington Library Collection, 69416.

Notes to Chapter Four

1. See Donna B. Hamilton, *Virgil and The Tempest: The Politics of Imitation*, (Columbus, Ohio, 1989).

2. R. C. Fulton comments on the traditional classical iconography in the betrothal masque in "*The Tempest*: The Masque of Iris, Ceres, and Juno" in *Shakespeare and the Masque*, gen. ed. Stephen Orgel (New York, 1988), 120–78. Gary Schmidgall in *Shakespeare and the Courtly Aesthetic* (Berkeley, 1981) has called attention to elements in *Hymenaei* that suggest "more than a casual relation" with *The Tempest*; namely, "contentious music"in *Hymenaei* reflecting "confused noise" in act 4 of Shakespeare's play; the "descent of Juno" in both works; Caliban's and Prospero's comments on sounds and visions like comments found in Jonson's masque; and a circle dance in the masque that reflects the circle Prospero draws in act 5. Schmidgall notes too that "in both works "*pietas* crushes *furor*; in both, potent virtue renders vice impotent." He adds that "magic was a common theatrical means of effecting the representation of this bias" (224–25). See also the account of the iconography in *Hymenaei* in D. J. Gordon, "Jonson's Masque of Union," *The Renaissance Imagination*, ed. Stephen Orgel (Berkeley, 1975), 157–84.

3. *The Vision of the 12. Goddesses*, presented in a Maske the 8. of Ianuary, at Hampton Court (London: Printed by T. C. for Simon Waterson, 1604), unnumbered page.

4. Campion, *The Description of a Maske*: Presented in the Banqueting roome at Whitehall . . . At the Marriage of the Right Honourable the Earle of Somerset (London: Printed by E. A. for *Lawrence Li'sle*, 1614), A 2r and v.

5. Daniel, *Tethys Festival*, E 2.

6. See remarks on the identifications of Prospero and other characters in *The Tempest: A New Variorum Edition*, (1892, reprint New York, 1964); Hallett Smith's "*The Tempest* as a Kaleidoscope," 1–2; Michael Srigley, *Images of Regeneration*, 116–40; and Glynne Wickham, "Masque and Anti-masque in *The Tempest*," 2–5. See also A. D. Nuttall's discussion of how *The Tempest* combines "allegoristic" and metaphysical meaning in *Two Concepts of Allegory* (New York, 1957). G. Wilson Knight in his chapter "Myth and Miracle," in *The Crown of Life* (New York, London and Toronto, 1947), 17–28, makes the distinction that "Prospero is not God but Shakespeare—or rather the controlling judgement of Shakespeare, since Ariel and Caliban are also representations of dual minor potentialities of his soul." John Dover Wilson in *The Essential Shakespeare* (Cambridge, England, 1932), 131–45, maintains that Prospero has "much of Shakespeare himself in

him" with the Epilogue representing Shakespeare's "hinted farewell to the theatre."

7. See Alwin B. Kernan, *The Playwright as Magician: Shakespeare's Image of the Poet in the English Public Theater* (New Haven and London, 1975); and Jackson Cope, *The Theater and the Dream: from Metaphor to Form in Renaissance Drama* (Baltimore, 1973).

8. T. G. Bishop in *Shakespeare and the Theatre of Wonder* (Cambridge, England, 1996), 176–77, rightly focuses on the original and often unsettling quality of the play and its symbolism in observing that "Shakespeare's evocations of wonder," particularly in *The Winter's Tale* and *The Tempest*, "are profoundly transactional, delicate, and full of difficult turbulences." But Bishop draws too sharp a differentiation between Jonson's masques with, in his words, their "fixed" "intellectual content" and "metaphoric trappings for the evocation of a set response," and what he terms Shakespeare's "deep psychology of metaphor" which, he says, produces unexpected results. Shakespeare, Bishop maintains, rejects both the "coercive in its spectacular articulation" and the sublimation of "conflict into a polarity of images."

9. In *Somerset's Masque*, for example, there appears a traditional, strictly typal antic figure, the "*Ayre*," who dances "In a skye-coloured skin coate, with a mantle painted with Fowle, and on his head an Eagle. . . ." Another typal antic spirit, the "*Earth*," dances as well, dressed "in a skin coate of grasse greene, a mantle painted full of trees, plants and flowers. And on his head an oake growing" (B recto).

Notes to Chapter Five

1. *The Memorable Masque* . . . As it was performed before the king, at White-Hall on Shroue Munday at night; being the 15 of February, 1613. At the Princely celebration of the most Royall *Nuptialls of the* Palsgraue, *and his trice graious Princess* Elizabeth. &c (London: Printed by G. Eld, for George Norton, 1613).

2. Thomas More, *Utopia*, ed. Edward Surtz (New Haven, 1964); and the utopian comments in the "Democritus Junior to the Reader" segment of Robert Burton's *The Anatomy of Melancholy* eds. Floyd Dell and Paul Jordan-Smith (New York, 1955), 83–93.

3. See Jonson's masques *Hymenaei* and *The Golden Age Restored* in *Ben Jonson*, 7.208–41, 419–29. The theme of the return of a Golden Age appeared also in Thomas Heywood's pageant play *The Golden Age* (1611). The repeated and very popular representation of ideal Arcadian and Golden Age themes in Stuart

and Caroline court theatricals has been treated in Erica Veevers, *Images of Love and Religion: Queen Henrietta Maria and Court Entertainments* (Cambridge, England, 1989); and in the citing of Arcadian figures and iconography by John Harris, Stephen Orgel, and Roy Strong, *The King's Arcadia: Inigo Jones and the Stuart Court* [a printed catalogue for a 1973 exhibition at the Masquing House] (London, 1973). See also the discussion of seventeenth century millenarian tracts in E. V. Tuveson, *Millennium and Utopia* (Berkeley and Los Angeles, 1949).

4. See *The Masque of Blacknesse* and *Newes From the New World Discover'd in the Moon* in *Ben Jonson*, 7.167–89, 512–25. See also Thomas Campion, "The Description of a Maske, Presented before the Kinge Maiestie *at White-Hall, on Twelfth Night* last, in honour of the Lord Hayes, and his Bride, Daughter and Heire to the Honourable the Lord Dennye" (London: Imprinted by John Wilndet for John Brown, 1607).

5. *John Milton*, 45–46, ll. 93–105.

6. See the passages in Matthew, together with Mark 15.33 and Luke 23.44, in Bibles popular in England during the period; namely, the *Geneva Bible* (London: Rouland Hall, 1560); *The holy Byble, conteynying the olde and newe Testament Set foorth by authoritie*, Bishop's Version (London: Richard Jugge, 1575); and *The Bible: Holy Scripture*, Geneva Version (London: Christopher Barker, 1576).

7. See King James's comments on magicians in league with the devil in *Daemonologie in forme of a Dialogue*, xii. In this text, the figure Epistemon, a spokesman for the king's views, does admit that some persons have simply studied magic without entering "themselues in Sathans seruice," but he immediately adds that such persons are nevertheless dangerously exposed to the devil's "baites" and so may fall into his hands. In a central statement that would appear unmistakably to reflect what is known of the king's own opinions, Epistemon then condemns the actual "practise" of magic as an "offense" against God (15). In *Daemonologie* James even denounced the conjurer-diplomat Girolamo Scotto who had performed card tricks for Queene Elizabeth and who had occasionally served as an ambassabor for the occultist Holy Roman Emperor Rudolf II, the ruler with whom Frederick was consulting in 1611 at the approximate time the English marriage was announced. The king also dismissed from court and did not patronize the Queen's former advisor, Dr. John Dee, who was part occultist, part mathematician, part navigational expert, and part charlatan.

See also Frances Yates's studies of occult influences in England and in the English court in *Giordano Bruno and the Hermetic*

Tradition (Chicago, 1969); *The Occult Philosophy in the Elizabethan Age* (London, 1979); and *The Rosicrucian Enlightenment* (London, 1972). See also Colin Still, *Shakespeare's Mystery Play*, revised as *The Timeless Theme*; Michael Srigley, *Images of Regeneration*; and Christopher McIntosh, *The Rosy Cross Unveiled: The History, Mythology and Rituals of an Occult Order* (Wellingborough, 1980). R. W. Rowse in *Sex and Society in Shakespeare's Age: Simon Forman the Astrologer* (New York, 1974) examines the relationship between Forman, the astrologer and magician, and the French Huguenot couple, the Montjoies, in whose house on Silver Street Shakespeare lived in 1602, and probably before and after that year.

Notes to Epilogue

1. "A short discourse," *Critical Essays of the Seventeenth Century*, ed. J. E. Spingard, vol. 2, (Oxford, 1908), 95.

2. The transformation of literary as well as theatrical forms in the seventeenth century can be traced in Dryden's further activities. In 1673 Dryden registered with the Stationer *The Fall of Angells, and man in innocence, an heroick opera*, a theatrical adaptation of Milton's epic *Paradise Lost.* Milton had originally conceived of this work on the Fall as a sacred representation, a closet drama, giving it the title "Adam Unparadized" and writing four outlines. Milton's nephew, Edward Phillips, in his *Life of Milton* tells of hearing his uncle in the 1640s recite lines from the new work which Phillips calls a "drama." Milton finally published his poem in 1667 as a 10-book epic, and then again in 1674, with 15 lines added, as a 12-book epic. In a dedicatory poem in the 1674 edition, Andrew Marvell writes of his fear that the epic will be transformed into "Scenes" and shown "in a Play." In 1677, Dryden did indeed write and publish a drama, adapted from the epic, under the title *The State of Innocence and Fall of Man.* See Marvell's dedecatory poem and Phillips's *The Life of Milton* in *John Milton*, 209, 1030.

Index